A Christmas Journey

*A Collection Of Resources
For Advent
And Christmas*

**Alan E. Siewert
H. Michael Nehls
Judy Gattis Smith
Jennifer Hockenbery Dragseth
Rod Tkach**

CSS Publishing Company, Inc., Lima, Ohio

A CHRISTMAS JOURNEY

An Unlikely Cast is a revised edition of the booklet published by CSS Publishing Company, Inc., in 1976, ISBN 0-89536-245-7.

The Colors Of Christmas is a revised edition of the booklet published by CSS Publishing Company, Inc., in 1978, ISBN 0-89536-838-2.

Is This The Road To Bethlehem? is a revised edition of the booklet published by CSS Publishing Company, Inc., in 1978, ISBN 0-89536-343-7.

For more information about CSS Publishing Company resources, visit our website at www.csspub.com or email us at custserv@csspub.com or call (800) 241-4056.

Cover Design by Barbara Spencer
ISBN-13: 978-0-7880-2405-4
ISBN-10: 0-7880-2405-1   PRINTED IN U.S.A.

Table Of Contents

An Unlikely Cast

Dramatic Monologues For Advent

Alan E. Siewert

Introduction

One might easily label the season of Advent as the "beginning of God's Holy Drama." As such, Advent is unique in that it recalls to our minds an "unlikely cast of characters." After all, here is God's wonderful, decisive action on behalf of humankind, and look at those who are active in its unfolding: a young Nazarene maiden, a humble carpenter, common shepherds, and the like.

Certainly, one would think that God could have chosen better, more appropriate characters to usher in the beginning of the New Covenant! There were persons of higher social position, individuals esteemed by the religious, political, and economic sectors of the society at that time. And, certainly, there were more illustrious locations for the staging of the drama than was the case with such places as tiny Bethlehem and Nazareth. Why this "unlikely cast of characters"?

Most assuredly, the wonder and amazement that surrounds Advent is elicited by these surprising characters. The "unlikely cast" indicated dramatically that the Messiah was coming for *all* people. With God, nothing was impossible. He could utilize the most mundane circumstances and the most common people to accomplish his purposes. Within this fact lies the true magnificence of the meaning of the season of Advent. If God could work through such people as those so many years ago, then he can still do great things through us today! Advent should be a time when we grow to appreciate the simple wonder of God's activity. The characters were people with whom the most common of us today can identify. This collection of dramatic monologues is dedicated to the hope that we can recapture the simple wonder of Advent, and bring to life that unlikely cast of characters.

The use of drama, particularly character portrayals, needs no defense for those of you who have already been exposed to this medium. It provides deep insight into the characters, which otherwise might only be dull sermon material. It exposes congregations to the reality of emotions, problems, and the circumstances surrounding biblical events. It also furnishes a means whereby people can significantly identify with God's activity. Otherwise common events, events taken for granted, literally jump from the pages and become real, something to be experienced.

The following monologues are designed to be used for mid-week Advent services, special programs, or even Sunday morning worship. The scope of their use is limited only by your imagination and ingenuity.

In all cases, it is suggested that worship services or programs into which the monologues are to be incorporated be kept at a minimum. For best effect, the monologue should be the main focal point.

Prior to each monologue text itself, there is an appropriate scripture reading which may serve effectively as a gospel reading preceding the presentation. The use of a few hymns and complementary responsive readings is also encouraged.

Specific staging and costuming notes precede each monologue text. These, however, should not be regarded as absolutes ... use your own ingenuity! In general, the main scene of activity should revolve around a centrally located lectern in the chancel or stage area. Memorization of the texts does, of course, enhance effectiveness. However, prepared sections of the script may well be placed at various locations to provide for movement within the delivery. Needless to say, frequent rehearsal is vitally important.

Now, for a general word concerning makeup and costumes. Certainly, one's attention should be focused mainly upon "getting into character," knowing the text well, being able to be expressive. Simple costuming, however, also helps to "sell" the character to yourself as well as to your audience. Simple flowing robes, sandals, a wig, and the like, can do wonders for putting you into character. Where beards are suggested, they may be created easily and inexpensively by using crepe hair and latex cement, available at most costume or theatrical supply stores, as well as from high school or college drama departments. Once assembled, the beards may be used repeatedly.

One final note: Allow yourself plenty of time in preparation. Involve the laity! Rather than presenting a whole series of the monologues during one Advent season, you may wish to limit your efforts to one well-done portrayal, merely providing a little variety in your regular worship format.

I sincerely hope that you will find the medium of the dramatic monologues to be as rewarding to you and your congregation as I have found.

Alan E. Siewert

Joseph — The Stepfather

Now the birth of Jesus Christ took place in this way. When his mother Mary had been betrothed to Joseph, before they came together she was found to be with child of the Holy Spirit; and her husband Joseph, being a just man and unwilling to put her to shame, resolved to divorce her quietly. But as he considered this, behold, an angel of the Lord appeared to him in a dream, saying, "Joseph, son of David, do not fear to take Mary your wife, for that which is conceived in her is of the Holy Spirit; she will bear a son, and you shall call his name Jesus, for he will save his people from their sins." All this took place to fulfil what the Lord had spoken by the prophet: "Behold, a virgin shall conceive and bear a son, and his name shall be called Emmanuel" (which means, God with us). When Joseph woke from sleep, he did as the angel of the Lord commanded him; he took his wife, but knew her not until she had borne a son; and he called his name Jesus. — Matthew 1:18-25

In this monologue, Joseph is portrayed as a man caught up in his thoughts. Occasionally engulfed in reverie, without directly addressing the audience, Joseph "talks to himself" about the events which have recently changed his life. He evidences a variety of moods, ranging from anguish, to deep questioning, to joy.

Joseph's costume may be simply created. He may be bearded, wearing a simple, white robe (perhaps an alb or choir robe), a colorful waist sash, a solid-colored piece of material draped over his shoulders, and sandals. An added realistic effect may be created if Joseph holds a wooden mallet in his hand.

If a hymn is sung prior to the presentation, Joseph should take his place before the completion of the hymn's last stanza. He should be seated in a chair either in front of or alongside the central lectern. Joseph should be mobile in his thoughtfulness. He should be quite explicit in the expressions of his emotions.

*   *   *

Oh — *(in anguish, rising from chair)* — those who say that real problems and harsh decisions are reserved for kings and princes — Ha! — I wish, then, that they would have had these problems of mine to contend with over the past agonizing months! Why has all this fallen upon me? I am not an evil person. I am certainly no king, no prince! Then, why all this soul-searching confusion for me — a Nazarene carpenter? Why me, Joseph?

(with much animation) With my skill, why couldn't I have built a fortress for myself — protecting me from this dilemma? But then it would also have secluded me from any joy. Before, days were so wonderful to me. I loved my work, and that love was visible — creating beauty and usefulness out of fine wood. My tiny shop was my sanctuary from the pain of the world. I could hammer and carve my frustrations away. But now, I can't eat or sleep. I can't work the way I should. The events of these past months constantly divert my attention. They have, at times, literally haunted me.

Oh, Mary — my beautiful, sweet, innocent Mary! I constantly see the joy and radiance in your life as you carry that child. It is a stark contrast to the feelings that rack me constantly, and I wonder if we would be engaged now, if I could have seen at least this far into the future. This has not been an easy time for me. I wonder if you, Mary, know what I have been going through. I lie awake, wondering if you know how many times I have gone over the events in my mind, talking to myself as I do now.

I have been left with little else but my thoughts, and they seem so vivid, so alive to me. *(deeply pensive)* How beautiful you always were when you would come to the well. And how sly I was to steal glances at you from my carpenter's cell. When our eyes finally did meet — the attraction, the magic. It was as if our hearts were joined in a beautiful dance! What a wonderful feeling! It was as if, in one glance, you had made my life complete.

Perhaps I did act too impulsively that day when I gathered my witnesses — the day I publicly gave you that gift, sealing our engagement, announcing my intention to make you my wife. According to our custom, from that day on, our village considered us as man and wife, even though the ceremony had not taken place —

even though we were for some time to share nothing more than those glances and a few words.

Oh, Mary, I was so happy that day! I could hardly do my day's work; I was so filled with joy. As I prayed that night, I thanked God, the God of our fathers. I thanked him for his blessings — for you! Little did I know that that prayer of thanks would soon turn into a cry of dismay — a cry, "Why, God? — Why am I being punished in such a way?"

That day when I learned that you were pregnant, Mary — was the day when all my present troubles began! People, good friends, thinking that this was *my* child, and I knowing that this was not so. Oh, Mary, the thoughts that went through my mind! They were natural concerns, for I really did not know you that well. Could I live with an unfaithful woman — a woman whose wedding gift to me would be a child not of my own flesh? And, to accentuate it all the more, could I live with someone who seemed to have such joy over this fact? Those thoughts, Mary — those thoughts!

I had always been a good Jew, a devout servant of God in my own humble manner, submitting my life to the standards of the Law of Moses. I was tempted, even resolved at one point, to follow the way of the law; to give you a letter of divorce, breaking our betrothal, even before our marriage was to be consummated. No one would have condemned me for such an action, for this was the way of the law and common to our heritage. But, oh, I knew what this would mean for you, Mary — to be branded as unclean, an adulteress, condemned for the rest of your life. To complicate the matter all the more, I could not deny the fact that I loved you.

I was constantly haunted by your apparent joy over the life that you carried within you. Instead of cowering in shame, your life seemed more fulfilled, openly radiant, as if you knew something grand and wonderful that no one else in all the world knew. You certainly did not convey the image of the sad, heartbroken, unwed mother-to-be. Frankly, your joy haunted me! Oh, yes, I really did strongly consider that letter of divorce. In fact, it was while I deeply contemplated that course of action that God's message came to me in a dream — a dream which made less frightening the nightmare that I was living.

As a devout Jew, I was not ignorant of the fact that our Messiah, the Savior of Israel, had been promised to be of the ancestry of our great King David — my ancestry! The prophets had spoken of the coming of a grand and glorious king, a king who would restore us truly as God's people. A king was to come, and I imagined him one day being born into a royal family, arrayed with shimmering robes, wearing a golden-jeweled crown.

But, then that dream, the message of God himself — the announcement which continually echoes in my mind: "Joseph, son of David, do not fear to take Mary your wife, for that which is conceived of her is of the Holy Spirit; she will bear a son, and you shall call his name Jesus, for he will save his people from their sins." Almost unbelievable those words seemed to me!

Yet, upon hearing them, I knew why you were so radiant, so happy, Mary. You already were aware of all of this. You knew the truth behind the heavenly message. You were already living the truth. You knew what this new life was all about! You knew that you were to be the mother of the Savior of Israel!

After God's announcement to me, for some reason, my mind seemed to be unchained. So much became clear. I could remember Isaiah's ancient prophecy: "Behold, a virgin shall conceive and bear a son, and his name shall be called Emmanuel, which means 'God with us.' "

But, I thought: We are such humble people — a carpenter and his young wife! How can this be happening to us? Certainly, the Messiah would be born into more elegant circumstances than what we could offer. Then I remembered how God had often worked through unlikely people to accomplish great things — Jacob, Moses, and the shepherd-king, David. As a carpenter, even I have learned how the most beautiful things can be fashioned from rough and common elements. Who am I to assume that I am a more skillful craftsman than God?

Perhaps, however, I am thinking only about things that lessen the pain of these present circumstances. But, no — the vision, the message from God. That was as real as my thoughts are today.

Is it possible that I am to be the guardian of God's Messiah? He is not of my flesh, but certainly he will grow up calling me

"Father." God said that this one will save his people from their sins, but certainly he will establish a magnificent earthly kingdom. We have waited so long for that promised king to free us from our bondage and restore us to a favored position with God. What position will I have in that kingdom? How will the scribes record my participation?

Well, now, enough of this idle dreaming. There are real problems to be faced, threatening to confound our plans. Now everything is so difficult — the child soon to be born, and we must travel from Nazareth to Bethlehem, according to the order issued by the authority of Caesar Augustus, to be enrolled for taxation. Some might not see this as such a great problem; after all, the command is only directed to the heads of households, but how can I leave Mary now? Certainly, the child would be born while I was away. I cannot leave her alone to face the scorn and contemptuous glances of the villagers.

Perhaps I want to believe it all so much — this great event to happen — that I can only remember things that support me in my confusion. Here we are, however, preparing to travel to Bethlehem, knowing full well that this glorious stepson of mine will, in all probability, be born in that out-of-the-way village. And, I can only remember the words of the prophet Micah: "And you, O Bethlehem — from you shall come a ruler who will govern my people Israel."

Oh, Lord, if only this could be so! *(begins to exit)* If only this could be so!

Mary — The Favored One

And he came to her and said, "Hail, O favored one, the Lord is with you!" But she was greatly troubled at the saying, and considered in her mind what sort of greeting this might be. And the angel said to her, "Do not be afraid, Mary, for you have found favor with God." ... And Mary said, "My soul magnifies the Lord, and my spirit rejoices in God my Savior, for he has regarded the low estate of his handmaiden. For behold, henceforth all generations will call me blessed; for he who is mighty has done great things for me, and holy is his name." — Luke 1:28-30, 46-49

The portrayal of Mary should be presented by a young woman. The character should evidence great inner joy and peace, yet in a humble fashion. Her general tone should be one of amazement over the fact that she has been "so favored."

Entering from the chancel door or from the side of the stage, Mary joyfully approaches the center lectern. Her costume might well consist of a flowing, white robe, along with a white or light blue mantel, covering her head and draped over her shoulders. Although not lifelessly chained, Mary's discourse by and large will be from the center lectern. As an additional visual aid, Mary might carry some cloths to be referred to as the "swaddling cloths." Above all, as Mary ponders through the story she is relaying, she should frequently pause and smile as various things flash through her mind.

*   *   *

(in humble amazement) Me! — the mother of the Christ! To come to you with that title ascribed to me is still so amazing! I know what your thoughts must be, for they are thoughts not unfamiliar to me. Why should such favor be showered upon a humble Nazarene maiden — one so meek and so common?

True, I was not different from other girls my age. I liked to dream. I enjoyed peaceful walks in the meadows, rejoicing over

15

the beauty of the flowers, smelling the sweet aroma of nature's splendor. I worked and I played like others my age.

You will find nothing dramatic about my childhood history — nothing certainly that would foretell the position for which I was chosen. But, in all reality — my life, my history, did not begin until the Lord — the God of our fathers — touched my life.

I remember that night so vividly, a night like so many Palestinian nights — still and hot — when God sent his messenger to me. Arrayed in blinding radiance, he said to me: "Hail, O favored one, the Lord is with you." Oh, yes, I was greatly troubled, fearful, and curious about the manner in which I was greeted. Me, Mary — a favored one?

In the midst of my fearful trembling, this agent from God consoled me. Again he spoke: "Do not be afraid, Mary," he said, "for you have found favor with God. And, behold, you will conceive — and bear a son, and you shall call his name Jesus."

Even in the shock of that moment, my mind hummed with activity. I thought: What will this child be? Why will he be unlike other children? Why would God so purposefully announce his coming? And my thoughts were immediately responded to by the messenger, as he said: "He will be great, and will be called the Son of the Most High; and the Lord will give to him the throne of his father David, and he will reign over the house of Jacob for ever; and of his kingdom there will be no end."

My friends, you can well imagine the amazement that I felt! This news, however, was so hard to accept. I had no husband. Oh, I was betrothed to gentle Joseph, the carpenter. Surely, if this son of mine was to be the great deliverer, the hoped-for Messiah, his father would have to be a prince — royalty of our nation — and not a humble working craftsman! It was all so confusing, but, as if sensing my confusion, the relayer of God's will said to me: "The Holy Spirit will come upon you, and the power of the Most High will overshadow you; therefore the child to be born will be called holy, the Son of God."

As unbelievable as it seemed, it all became much clearer with those words. This Messiah was not to be the same manner of king for whom our nation had been looking. God implied through his message to me that his Son — my son — God himself was to enter our lives. I had never dreamed of the Lord as being so caring, so filled with love, as was then being revealed to me. Why, we had always felt that God was distant, unapproachable, certainly not personal. And yet, look at what was happening to me! It seemed to be beyond possibility.

Still, the messenger responded to my apparent awe and disbelief. He said: "With God nothing is impossible!" Did you hear that? Nothing is impossible! I then submitted to the reality of the event and to God's will, saying: "Behold I am the handmaiden of the Lord; let it be to me according to your word." My life, my history, as you know it, had begun.

(pausing pensively, and then) My life was filled with joy and indescribable wonder for the next nine months. I had learned about a woman called Elizabeth who was experiencing the favor of the Lord. She was the wife of a priest, Zechariah, and she was well advanced in age. Her people regarded her as lowly, for she was without children, and to our people this was a sign of God's punishment. But rumor had it that God had blessed her with the ability to conceive even in her old age. I traveled to see Elizabeth — I suppose hoping that this would reinforce my faith in God's purpose for my own life.

Uncommon as the practice was, I left my betrothed, Joseph, and made the long, tedious journey into the hill country of Judah to see this blessed Elizabeth. Throughout the course of those eighty difficult miles, I pondered what had been revealed to me. Could God be active in such a way? Could I, Mary, be the recipient of such a blessing? The messenger's words echoed constantly in my thoughts — "With God nothing is impossible! With God nothing is impossible!"

(effervescently) Wonder of wonders! When I first met Elizabeth, beaming in elderly radiance, she greeted me as if she had always known me. I had come to honor her, and yet she welcomed me by saying, "Blessed are you among women, and blessed is the fruit of your womb!" And she immediately asked me, "And why is this granted me that the mother of my Lord should come to me?"

What I was confused about, she knew as fact! In spite of my uncertainty concerning my role, Elizabeth continued by saying, "Blessed is she who believed that there would be a fulfillment of what was spoken to her from the Lord."

(powerfully) I was completely overcome by the Spirit that God said would be part of me, and I said, "My soul magnifies the Lord, and my spirit rejoices in God my Savior, for he has regarded the low estate of his handmaiden." I found what I had hoped for. There were then no doubts. The three months that I remained with Elizabeth were joyful, and I became stronger, ever sensing the strength of her faith. The sojourn with Elizabeth was not without difficulty, but God granted me patience — such that I had never had before. You see, Zechariah could not speak. He made gestures, scribblings in the soil, by which he communicated with us. We sensed, as he already knew, that his affliction was a sign of God's activity about to be fulfilled in the birth of the child Elizabeth carried.

When the child, a son, was born to Elizabeth, I shared in the joy. When you have waited nearly a lifetime for something so wonderful — when you have had to bear the rejection of so many, as Elizabeth did — well, I'm sure that you can imagine how she felt. The people whom Zechariah served expected the newborn son to be named after his father or given a name common to the family. You should have seen their amazed looks when Elizabeth and Zechariah indicated that their son would bear the name John. In his speechless condition, Zechariah had scrawled upon a tablet these words, "His name shall be called John."

And, further amazement was kindled when, with this action, Zechariah's tongue was unchained and he praised God loudly and joyfully. He looked down upon his infant son, aware of his destiny, and said, "And you, child, will be called the prophet of the Most High; for you will go before the Lord to prepare his ways." Oh, yes, that's right; that tiny infant would one day be the one whom you know by the name of John the Baptist. *(pause)*

Strengthened in my commitment, firm in my faith, joyful in my purpose — I then journeyed back to Nazareth. The three months had passed quickly. That time, however, had made my own condition visible. I knew what surprise, what shock there would be for my betrothed, Joseph, for the life that I carried within me was evident. I knew that the rumors and the scorn of the people would not always be easy to bear. I was not surprised that Joseph looked upon me with some reproach and doubts about my character.

It was not easy for Joseph to think about the possibility of marrying a woman who would immediately offer him a stepson. Joseph had much inner struggling, even to the point of considering a letter of divorce. Alas, I could not fault him for his doubts. As I was to later learn, however, God had also revealed his plan to Joseph, and he accepted his role as stepfather with unshakable faith and dedication. God gave him strength and encouragement for this most difficult task.

For the next few months, the secret remained with us. As best we could, we tried to encourage one another. We thought and talked about the great prophets who had foretold the coming of the Messiah. Joseph was descended from the line of the great King David, and the prophets had said that the Savior would come from that ancestry. Even the great prophet, Isaiah, had relayed God's Word: "Behold, a virgin shall conceive and bear a son, and his name shall be called Emmanuel ... which means God with us." Certainly, we felt that it was true — God was with us!

We journeyed together in single-minded purpose to the town of Joseph's ancestry — Bethlehem. We were victims of the enrollment order issued by Caesar Augustus. We were victims, however, who would soon be used to usher in the greatest of victories.

I know that you have heard the details of that wonderful night so often. That night, of course, is the focal point of this time that you call Advent. The miracle of miracles happened. *(slowly, deliberately)* Huddled as comfortably as possible in that Bethlehem stable, I gave birth to my son, Jesus. I wrapped him in these *(display cloths)* simple cloths — hardly the garments of a king, are they? There was never really any doubt for me about his greatness. Elizabeth in her warmth, Joseph in his quiet confidence, the shepherds in their joyous adoration — they all confirmed God's message concerning that new life. My son was to be the Christ!

19

Perhaps many of you here know what I mean when I say that it is very hard for a mother to give up her son. And yet, I offer him to you. He has come for you. He, too, has regarded your low estate and has blessed you. I am his mother, but we are all his children. Yes, my son comes for you! *(exits)*

John — The Preparer

*But when he saw many of the Pharisees and Sadducees
coming for baptism, he said to them, "You brood of
vipers! Who warned you to flee from the wrath to come?
Bear fruit that befits repentance, and do not presume
to say to yourselves, 'We have Abraham as our father';
for I tell you, God is able from these stones to raise up
children to Abraham. Even now the axe is laid to the
root of the trees; every tree therefore that does not bear
good fruit is cut down and thrown into the fire. I baptize you with water for repentance, but he who is coming after me is mightier than I, whose sandals I am not
worthy to carry; he will baptize you with the Holy Spirit
and with fire. His winnowing fork is in his hand, and he
will clear his threshing floor and gather his wheat into
the granary, but the chaff he will burn with unquench-
able fire."*   — Matthew 3:7-12

John should be portrayed as a man with rough self-confidence.
Occasionally, in the midst of his discourse, his roughness shows
through, as does his tenderness in recalling the past.

John may appear with unkempt hair, a large, full beard, and
a rough, burlap tunic. A lining may be taken from an old full-
length coat to give the appearance of a garment made of camel's
hair. Leather remnants may be used to fashion a girdle (belt).
Sandals and a roughly hewn staff provide the finishing touch to
the costume.

Entering from a chancel or side stage door, John confidently
strides to the central lectern, shouting as he walks, "Repent! For
the kingdom of heaven is at hand!" John exits, loudly urging people
— according to the words of the last paragraph of the monologue
— to "prepare the way of the Lord," as he walks down the center
aisle.

*   *   *

(enter, shouting) Repent! For the kingdom of heaven is at hand! Please, my friends, do not be shocked by my rough language or appearance. They are parts of my life — difficult to forget or to cast aside.

I am John, known as "the Baptizer," and my life has not been marked by high fashion or by eloquent speech. Perhaps, by your standards, I resemble a street beggar or a rebel. Well, in my day, a beggar I was not, but to the Pharisees, I was definitely a rebel.

I assume that my message and my history are not unfamiliar to you. I have been pictured as a desert rat, stepping out from my solitude to call people to repentance — to a healthier relationship with God. Rough as my message seemed to many, beneath the message was my sincere belief that God was about to do something wonderful. I baptized people — any and all people — who wanted to show God that they were willing to turn from their sinful pasts.

And, I preached — I shouted that the kingdom of heaven was at hand, was within the reach of people. The kingdom was all wrapped up in a person — a man of whom I said that I was not even fit to be his slave. You call him the Christ — Jesus — and you gather here as you prepare to remember the event of his birth. You prepare to remember his arrival as an infant. I spent my life preparing people for his arrival as the king of their hearts.

Oh, I was not ignorant of his coming, his entrance into our world as the Bethlehem babe. My parents were all too aware of that miraculous event, and from the very time that I could understand, they told me all the details.

(pausing, thinking) I was born when my mother, Elizabeth, was well advanced in years. Her life had been hard, living in the hill country of Judah. And, it was made all the more difficult by her many barren years. For a woman to be without children — why, this was a sign of God's disfavor according to my people's traditional outlook — a sign hard to bear for any woman. But, it was all the more so for my mother, since she was the wife of a priest — my father, Zechariah.

Yet, in her old age, the God of our fathers had blessed my mother. For his miraculous mercy gave her the ability to bear a child. She often told me of the joy she experienced as she carried new life — me — within her. Her joy, however, was not confined to considering her own blessedness. Often, my old parents told the wonderful story to me, and each time it filled my heart with gladness and peace.

Apparently, a young, Nazarene maiden, known as Mary, had learned of God's show of favor upon my mother. And, filled with her own secret joy, Mary travelled the long, eighty miles from Nazareth to our home. As my mother frequently told, this young girl, too, had apparently found favor with the Lord, and my mother was aware — by God-given insight — of the greater blessing bestowed upon Mary. *(pensively)* Let me see now. I have heard these words so often — oh, yes, when Mary arrived, my mother exclaimed, "Blessed are you among women and blessed is the fruit of your womb." The picture painted by my mother is so vivid now. Mary was so amazed at the greeting she received! She had come to honor my mother-to-be, and yet she was the one being honored herself. My mother could sense her joy and the wonder of the event that was to come to pass through this young girl.

As I have been told, Mary remained with my mother for three months until the event of my birth. Mary's quiet confidence and her humble joy were a constant source of strength for the one who was to deliver me into the world. My father told me many times how much he appreciated the presence of Mary. His own acts of encouragement were limited to an endearing smile or a gentle touch. You see, my father, Zechariah, could not speak. His communications at that time were limited to gestures and scribblings in the soil. As my priest-father often told me, his affliction was a sign of God's activity about to be fulfilled in my birth.

During those three months that Mary resided with my parents, I guess that they frequently discussed the very practical problems that Mary faced. She, too, was to give birth to a son. God's messenger had relayed to her that the infant would be called Jesus — that he would be called holy, the Son of God — that he would be born of the power of the Holy Spirit — that he was to be the promised Messiah, whose kingdom would have no end.

Ah, yes, about those practical problems to which I referred. You see, Mary at that time had no husband. Oh, she was engaged to a humble carpenter from Nazareth — Joseph, by name. Mary was only human; she was concerned about Joseph's feelings. After all, should they be married, he would have to accept the fact that he would almost immediately become a stepfather. She feared that Joseph would label her as unclean, and that he might even secure a writ of divorce — that was customary according to our people's law — even before the wedding ceremony. As my mother told me, however, Mary grew in confidence. She seemed to sense that if God could do something so wonderful, as he was about to do through her, then her concerns were minor. She trusted completely in God's power.

When I was finally born, Mary was there to help and to share in my elderly parents' joy. As if it was not shock enough for the people of the area that my mother, Elizabeth, would deliver me in her old age — they were more amazed when I was given my name. You see, it is our people's custom that a son be named after his father or, at the very least, be given a name common to the family. From the very beginning, however, I imagine that my family knew that I would not lead a common life, according to tradition.

They called me John. This was surprising enough, but, as my father has said, our kinsmen were even more surprised by the manner in which he indicated what my name would be. In his speechless condition, their priest — Zechariah — had scrawled upon a tablet, "His name shall be called John." And, immediately upon doing this, what then happened has become popular legend. My father's tongue was unchained, and he praised God loudly and joyfully. As the story goes, he looked down upon me — his infant son — and said, "And you, child, will be called the prophet of the Most High; for you will go before the Lord to prepare his ways." *(pause)* He proclaimed my destiny before I could even understand the words. As my beloved mother often said, this declaration strengthened Mary all the more in her commitment.

I know that the rest of the story is familiar to you. Mary returned to Joseph at Nazareth. God saw them through their difficulties, and the One whom I was to preach about was born in Bethlehem.

Strange, isn't it, how God used what some might call such unlikely characters? Yes, it is still a source of amazement to me.

I spent my life preparing the hearts of people for his triumphant entrance. Now, you gather to prepare for his coming as the "infant king." I shouted in the wilderness, "Prepare the way of the Lord." And, I implore you now to realize that you are no more unlikely than I was to cry for and do the same thing.

Prepare a place for him in your hearts! He is the greatest treasure that humankind has even been given. That Bethlehem babe has become king of the universe!

(exits) Prepare the way of the Lord! He is the king who comes for you! Get ready to welcome him!

The Innkeeper

In those days a decree went out from Caesar Augustus that all the world should be enrolled. This was the first enrollment, when Quirinius was governor of Syria. And all went to be enrolled, each to his own city. And Joseph also went up from Galilee, from the city of Nazareth, to Judea, to the city of David, which is called Bethlehem, because he was of the house and lineage of David, to be enrolled with Mary, his betrothed, who was with child. And while they were there, the time came for her to be delivered. And she gave birth to her first-born son and wrapped him in swaddling cloths, and laid him in a manger, because there was no place for them in the inn. — Luke 2:1-7

This "no-name" visitor exhibits a great deal of defensiveness throughout his discourse. He should be portrayed as a shrewd businessman. The Innkeeper is rich in gestures, occasionally pointing at the audience, or slapping his coin-filled purse.

The Innkeeper's costume may be fashioned easily: a colorful tunic, a plain-colored sash and mantle (draped over his shoulder), a simple, leather purse with drawstrings (filled with coins, hanging from the sash), and sandals.

He enters slowly from the side or rear of the chancel, somewhat reluctant to address the gathering. His delivery mainly occurs from the center lectern, but he should exhibit some freedom of movement.

* * *

My visit with you, coming out from the past, may indeed seem strange to you. You might well ask, "What business does he have in approaching us? Why, he isn't even mentioned in our scriptures!" I do not deny that you are justified in questioning my appearance before you. My existence, as far as you are concerned, can be inferred only from the fact that it is stated in your holy writings that "there was no place for them in the inn."

26

You may well ask my name. So, go ahead — ask! But, the only answer that I can rightly give you is "Innkeeper." That's right — Innkeeper. I hope you can be content with that identity for me. I can see no reason why you should not; after all *(sarcastically)*, to the countless people who entered my humble establishment those many years ago, I had no identity other than that. I even had conditioned myself into forgetting my given name. My name was Innkeeper, and I was made aware of that constantly. *(shouting, with animation)* "Innkeeper, I want a lodging place!" "Innkeeper, bring more wine!" "Innkeeper, my plate is empty!" You see, my identity was hidden in the midst of the demands of my customers whom I was forced to serve.

When your place of business is in such a humble, lackluster town as Bethlehem, you learn to be very congenial. Your livelihood depends upon your ability to let indecencies and harsh demands roll off you like water off the back of a duck. You see, Bethlehem was by no means the entertainment spot of the Jewish world. Nestled in the rolling hills, about six miles south of mighty Jerusalem, my little Bethlehem was not much to behold. It was surrounded on all sides by the unglamorous flocks of those smelly, grazing sheep! Bethlehem was just a nice, quiet, little town — a fine place in which a family could settle quite comfortably, but not a very appealing location for a businessman such as I was. Oh *(mockingly)*, occasionally, the dreariness of daily life would be broken by the arrival of a caravan which had emerged from the desert. The common people enjoyed the wealth of their stories, but there was no wealth to be had for me. The caravan travelers would merely come into town to trade, to replenish their food stores, and then they would return to their beasts of burden to spend the night with them — not me!

Before that one, amazing night, Bethlehem's only claim to fame was that she had been the home of King David, and the scene of his anointment by the prophet Samuel. But, that certainly wasn't a drawing card for the tourist trade. It meant no coins for my purse.

Of course, even as an innkeeper, I was aware of the hopeful prophecy that surrounded tiny Bethlehem, and made her seem more important than she really was — to me, anyway! It was handed down to us that the prophet Micah had foretold: "But you, O Bethlehem Ephrathah, who are little to be among the clans of Judah, from you shall come forth for me one who is to be ruler in Israel, whose origin is from old, from ancient days." *(mockingly)* Nice words, huh? However, they certainly did not produce an air of expectancy in our little town. The prophecy did not bring interested spectators to our doorstep, waiting to see the arrival of the promised Messiah of whom Micah's words foretold. After all, those lovely words had been spoken some 800 years before Bethlehem was to see me as an innkeeper. Eight hundred years! No wonder there was no thrill of expectancy left! No wonder Bethlehem was not an attraction for the curious traveler!

Daily, I thought that fate had dealt me an ugly blow. Why, if I could have been born 800 years, or even 750 years sooner, I would probably have had a wonderful business. I wouldn't have had to beg for business. I would have been free from the morbid excitement I had exhibited when I heard that someone of prominence had died *(rub hands)* — greedily rubbing my hands, thinking that this would bring distant relatives and friends of the deceased to my inn, as they came to pay their last respects. Oh, yes, go right ahead and think what a terrible person I must have been, but I was fighting for my life! Wouldn't you *(pointing)* have thought and acted the same as I? You are business-oriented, practical people. You know all too well what I am talking about. *(pause)*

To say the least, I — like other people — lived in fear at that time, because we lived or, best put, existed under the controlling hand of the Roman Empire — those pagan dogs! The only beneficial thing about living in tiny Bethlehem was that we were somewhat ignored by the Roman scourge. We, however, were not immune to the mockery of Rome's bigoted power. Occasionally, patrols of soldiers would make their way into our midst, and fear gripped our tiny community. *(strongly)* Those Roman pigs would literally take over our lives. For me, their entrance would mean that I would be compelled to dole out food, lodging, and wine — knowing that I would receive but a token, if anything at all. They had no respect for our traditions, our faith, and no respect for any measure of human decency. I was all but bankrupt as it was, and I did not need their further drain on my meager resources. *(pause)*

Ha! How ironic that the orders of Rome that had brought so much misery in the past should, on one occasion, bring me such good fortune. From his distant, imperial throne *(sarcastically)*, the "great" Caesar Augustus had authorized a census of his subjects, when Quirinius reigned as governor over the northern province of Syria. Although our tiny nation was already overburdened with Roman-initiated taxes, it was apparently not sufficient for the greedy hand of Rome. They wanted more! The order was issued that all the heads of households had to return to the home of their ancestors to be enrolled for the purposes of taxation. This stirred up a furor among the Jews throughout the whole country!

It was a sweet surprise to me! It was as if Rome was about to repay me for all the pilfering of my resources. People, strangers, tourists — *customers* poured into insignificant little Bethlehem. They all represented coins to me — money for lodging — money for food and drink. For once in my hapless business life, I could bargain. Rich men, if they wanted my services, had to, and could afford to, pay the price. I sold space to the highest bidder; food was served at a premium. My purse *(slap purse)* rang with the sweet sound of silver! Caesar had become my friend — Ha! — imagine that — my friend! We were partners in a booming business! I felt no qualms about getting rich as a result of the misfortune of my countrymen. *(points)* Don't look at me so blankly. You know what I mean! *(pause)*

In the midst of all my profitable joy, a young couple approached me about securing lodging. The girl was very young, perhaps about fifteen years of age, and she looked very drawn and pregnant as she remained perched upon that donkey, while her husband addressed me. He called himself Joseph, and said that it was of the greatest necessity for them to find lodging as his wife, Mary, was near the time of delivery. Now *(appealing to audience)*, what would you have done if you had been in my position? Why, I would have had to turn out one of my fine, high-paying customers to make room for them, and they, very obviously, could not pay as much as the others. "There is no room in the inn," I told them.

Amazingly enough, they did not argue with me like the others. They were all too willing to accept my discouraging announcement. There was something quietly confident about them, in spite of their circumstances. Well, I have a heart, too. I directed them to a stable where the animals of many of my customers were housed, and there they made provision for their night's lodging.

Deafened by the merriment of my drunken guests, I did not hear the sound that night of new life entering into the world. I did not know that the infant cries which I missed would one day proclaim the greatest news that humankind was ever to hear. I did see those ragamuffin shepherds pressing to enter the stable, as if there was something worthy of adoration there. I can remember thinking, why would they leave their flocks untended on such a night as this, with so many strangers converging upon our little area? Little did I know that they had come to see the "Great Shepherd." How could I possibly have known that this whole episode was the very fulfillment of Micah's ancient prophecy? Only later was I to learn the reality of that. *(pause)*

Yes, I was the innkeeper, and I have a word for you. Don't be blinded the way I was by my desire to become wealthy. The child, born that night, who was later to be known as the Christ, offers wealth far beyond that symbolized by the sound *(grasp purse)* of silver.

You Christians call this time Advent, a time to remember the arrival of your Savior. Don't do as I did, denying him entrance. Be better innkeepers than I was — realize what and who is important. Open the doors of your hearts, and bid him enter. Don't bankrupt your lives by saying, "I have no room for you." *(exits)*

Meisha — The Shepherd

And in that region there were shepherds out in the field, keeping watch over their flock by night. And an angel of the Lord appeared to them, and the glory of the Lord shone around them, and they were filled with fear. And the angel said to them, "Be not afraid; for behold, I bring you good news of a great joy which will come to all the people; for to you is born this day in the city of David a Savior, who is Christ the Lord. And this will be a sign for you: you will find a babe wrapped in swaddling cloths and lying in a manger." And suddenly there was with the angel a multitude of heavenly host praising God and saying, "Glory to God in the highest, and on earth peace among men with whom he is pleased!"
— Luke 2:8-14

Meisha is a common, humble man. (There is no particular significance in the name Meisha.) Occasionally, he exhibits quiet confidence and pride.

His costume should be as simple and plain as he is: sandals, a plain, white robe, a piece of material draped over his head, and a shepherd's crook.

The shepherd enters from the rear or side of the chancel area and takes his position at the central lectern. His movement, utilizing the crook, will aid the effectiveness of the presentation. Meisha exits down the center aisle, saying the last paragraph of the script.

* * *

I know you have had more illustrious visitors to address you; so, please be tolerant of this *(points to self)* humble shepherd. My name is Meisha. My father and his fathers before him tended the flocks in the hill country of Judea.

Oh, I know that you, today, might regard my life's work with low esteem — an unexciting existence. Perhaps that is the case, by your standards. But, what is more wonderful than living close to

31

God's nature — to see the simple glory of life each day? You, today, miss so many of God's miracles.

A lowly shepherd — that I am. And yet, my roots stretch deep into the very beginnings of our people — the Israelites. Our nation, the chosen people of God, was born out of wandering, nomadic shepherds. I may sound defensive, but recall with me the great ones of our past, whose beginnings were no more glamorous than mine. Our forefather, Jacob, was a shepherd, as was Moses when he gave up his allegiance to Egypt. David was the great shepherd-king, and there was even the prophet Amos who tended the flocks. Proud in my low estate? Yes, I am!

Why, in the early days of my people, those smelly sheep — that you might regard with disfavor — represented the chief wealth and total livelihood. Those fragile creatures provided food, milk, and wool for clothing and covering for tents. Our flocks were our money. Many an important diplomatic decision was sealed with the exchange of flocks and fine, white wool. *(pause)*

As a nation, our covenant agreement with God was based on the law. God had provided a means of obtaining forgiveness through animal sacrifices, and many of those frail creatures we tended became burnt offerings, sin offerings, guilt offerings, and peace offerings.

Many of what you know as the psalms came from the shepherd-king, David. Tending his flocks in the same hills where I spent my life, David composed many hymns of praise to the God of our fathers. Beautiful words! Words that told about the greatness of our God. Oh, does that stir your memory a little? Remember David's song: "The Lord is my shepherd. I shall not want; he makes me lie down in green pastures ..." Ah, yes, I can see that is familiar to you. And you see, David even said that God was like a shepherd! So, do you wonder still why I am so proud of my position?

And, God said that we — his people — were like sheep that he wanted to gather unto himself. He once spoke through the prophet Ezekiel and said, "Behold, I, I myself, will search for my sheep, and will seek them out."

Can you now be more tolerant of my life's work? *(proudly)* Look at that history! It may be amazing to you, but I do stand before you — proud! *(pause)* But, alas, I would only be fair if I told you everything. History does show some unpleasantness. My people were subjected to captivity, and later to the scourge of Roman domination. We had the customs of others imposed upon us. Cities, trading, crafts, and the like became more important than the simple life of the pastoral shepherd. Values changed, and people forgot about their humble beginnings. Pride in our past was replaced by greed, and many of us shepherds became forgotten people.

Oh, yes, our lives were not exciting. We were chained to our flocks. You see, sheep are defenseless. They needed our constant care and protection. Left unguarded, our flocks would be ravaged by beasts and beast-like robbers. Our constant vigilance was called for, both day and night. We would spend the daylight hours with our weak charges, eating our midday meal alone, in their company.

The highlight of a day — to be sure, modest by your standards — would be a night's gathering with fellow shepherds. Huddled around a fire, which also served to ward off beasts of prey, we would talk about the day's happenings. "I took some he-goats to the temple," one might say. There would be the quiet nods. Or, there might have been the birth of a child to discuss. Or, some might tell of the caravan that passed along the highway that led to Jerusalem. Or, the trading that was done in Bethlehem. But, the greatest treasure was to be with other human beings.

Occasionally, we would talk about the hoped-for coming of the Messiah, the Great Shepherd. We speculated about his power and glory. We wondered if our people would once again regard our humble origins with pride. *(pause)*

It was on a night such as that, many long years ago, that the wonder of wonders occurred. For days before, our peaceful countryside surrounding Bethlehem had been disturbed by strangers pouring into the town. News travels slowly to the isolated shepherd. But, we had heard finally that our captors — Rome herself — had ordered that people return to the home of their ancestors to enroll for a census and more taxation.

Those were fearful days. Sheep are not equipped to withstand much turmoil. We worried that our flocks would be ravaged by robbers. We were constantly on guard.

On that evening, as we told each other of the day's happenings and the ceaseless variety of strange intruders, our lives were to be changed forever. For, suddenly, the light of our flickering fire seemed to grow to blinding brilliance. We strained and rubbed our eyes. It was as if the sun had come down and settled in our midst, and we were filled with great fear!

And then a voice, one we had never heard before, spoke to us, shaking the ground upon which we reclined. And we heard these words: "Be not afraid; for behold, I bring you good news of a great joy which will come to all the people; for to you is born this day in the city of David a Savior, who is Christ the Lord."

I wondered: Could it be that the promised, hoped-for Messiah was making his entrance into the city destined by the prophets to be his home? It seemed too wonderful to be true! *(pause)*

And, we were further told, "And this will be a sign for you: you will find the babe wrapped in swaddling cloths and lying in a manger." Oh, it cannot be, I thought — a manger for a king! But, my thoughts were interrupted by a most glorious sound. It was as if the whole world was singing — "Glory to God in the highest and on earth peace among men with whom he is pleased."

In spite of the danger — in spite of the night — in spite of the strangers, we looked at one another, saying with our eyes — as well as with our lips — that we must go into Bethlehem to see this wonder that had happened. And, as sheep, then being called by a greater shepherd, we were led to the place where the newborn child lay. There, as we had been told, we found that precious gift, hovered over by his mother, Mary, and her husband, Joseph.

(joyfully) We were filled with the wonder of the heavenly message and the sight of this infant Messiah-to-be — and, leaving, we told everyone we met what God was doing. *(pause)*

Lowly shepherds? Yes! And yet, God had chosen us to receive this great news. The shepherds became the sheep. *(enthusiastically)* Oh, and this is great news for you *(pointing)*, my friends! You can't fool me. I know that many of you regard yourselves as lowly, unimportant. But, his message is for you — as it was for us — for all people!

(exit down center aisle) God loves us all so much that he wants to gather us unto himself. Let him be your shepherd. Let the advent of the Messiah make a difference in your life! He can lead you to green pastures. He can make your life like the shepherd's psalm. Your Great Shepherd has come — for you!

The Colors
Of Christmas

*Six Sermons
And Object Lessons
For Advent And Christmas*

H. Michael Nehls

Preface

"The Colors Of Christmas" is a program of worship services designed for the local congregation. It is for use during the Advent and Christmas seasons of the church year. Both the children's message and the adult sermon follow the specific color theme for the day. Altar hangings and paraments should follow the color theme, too, where this is possible.

Advent is a time of anticipation, a time of hope. As God's people in Christ, we look for the coming of Christ, our Lord, as the Babe of Bethlehem, as the Christ of Christmas. In a larger sense, we also look forward to Christ's coming again in glory.

In an attempt to better share the truths of this special season, I created the program, "The Colors Of Christmas." The idea first came to me on a Saturday morning, as I watched the women of our Altar Guild changing the paraments in the sanctuary. As the colors were changed, it came to me that Christmas is certainly a season of color. Why not, then, use the colors of the Advent/Christmas season to demonstrate the truths behind the great Gift of Christ in Christmas?

The children's message includes a ribbon to be worn of the color theme for the day. Inexpensive ribbon can be purchased at craft stores or discount stores. You will need to purchase three to four inches of ribbon per child, plus safety pins to put them on each child's attire. Each child was given a different ribbon each Sunday and I wore one on my robe, too. The children certainly looked forward to the different color ribbons and enjoyed the program very much. Each week, we added a new ribbon until we wore all six. Many of the children wore all six ribbons several weeks after the program was completed. Perhaps the leaders in the choir or a group of mothers could help put the ribbons on the children each week.

"The Colors Of Christmas" seeks to share the varied aspects of the birth, life, and glory of Jesus Christ, that God's people may prepare fully to celebrate his birth. To that end, I commend its use for others. May God alone be glorified.

H. Michael Nehls

Green

Good morning, boys and girls. During the morning announcements today, I told you what the special color is for this morning. Do you remember what it is? That's right, *green*. Green is the color for the day. And what day is today? That's right, today is the first Sunday of Advent, the beginning of a new church year. Today we also begin to think about Christmas, that time when we all celebrate the birth of God's Son, Jesus. Each Sunday during this Advent/Christmas season, we will have a different color as our theme. This morning, we begin with the color green.

Can you name some things that are green in color? Grass and leaves? Those are good answers. Green is the color of life, of growth. Each spring, we look forward to the greening of the grass and the coming again of the leaves and plants. When God first created the world, what color do you think it was? Yes, I think it was probably green, too.

But green is also one of the primary Christmas colors. Can you think of some special "green" things of Christmas? The Christmas tree is a good answer. It is an evergreen tree. It is always green, isn't it? Is there anything else that's green for Christmas? The Advent wreath! Very good. There are a few other things some of the adults might remember. Holly and mistletoe are popular during the Christmas season. All of these things, especially the Christmas tree, the evergreen, remind us that God has given us life. And with the coming of Christmas, God is about to give us new life again, through the birth of his baby Son, Jesus.

So that you will remember that, I have in my bag this morning a green ribbon for each of you to wear. Each Sunday during this Christmas season, you will receive a different color ribbon. I want you to wear them, adding each new color every Sunday. Here is a green ribbon for each of you, and there is even one for me to wear on my robe. Now, what does the color green remind us of? That's right; life and growth. God gives us life, in creation and in the birth of his Son, Jesus.

Green, The Color Of Life

Genesis 1:1-5; John 1:1-5

These two sections of scripture portray for us, in a panoramic way, the story of creation. Genesis teaches that in the beginning there was God who created all things. There was nothing in the beginning until God caused it to happen. He spoke, and creation became a reality. God created everything from nothing. And behold, it was very good!

In much the same way, John's Gospel also teaches us about creation. It begins just as the Genesis creation account: *In the beginning*. But John says more, proclaiming that God's own Son, the Word made flesh, Jesus, our Emmanuel, was involved in this act of creation. "Without him was not anything made that was made!" Jesus, then, is the one through whom all things were created. We recognize the truth that life comes from him. He is the source of life, all life. The creating life has come through his own hand, by his powerful Word. Eternal life has come through his own death and resurrection. Through creation, Christ has given us the gift of life. Through his passion, death, and resurrection, he has given that gift of life eternal. So this Holy Child of Bethlehem, this babe in the Christmas manger, is also the creating, omnipresent God. He, and he alone, is the source of all life, both in this world and the next.

Green is the color of life. That fact most assuredly pervades our thinking when we consider the colors of Christmas! In our outdoors this time of year, there is a marked lack of the color green. The leaves are gone. Most plants have died from frost and exposure. We are in the season of late autumn, early winter. This is a time of dormancy in the life of most growing things. They hibernate, they go to sleep, they die.

Now, of course, there is a highly technical, scientific explanation as to what actually happens. My college biology suggests that the chlorophyll dies and the carotene takes over, becoming pre-dominant. But, we're not scientists. We simply know that in autumn and winter, the plants die and the leaves fall. That's all we know, and probably all we need to know about such a subject. We're just people trying to understand life ... the gift of life given to us by Christ himself.

But, one of the most important colors of Christmas is green. We see that "green" and that "greenery" surrounding us at Christmas. Today, we see it here, in God's house, the church. We find it in our green paraments: on the altar, lectern, and pulpit, in the color of my stole and in my cross, in the ribbons of life we gave the youngsters a few moments ago. And we also see green in the holly and mistletoe of the yuletide season. Our Advent wreath is green, and our Christmas tree and decorations in the sanctuary themselves will abound with green.

A good symbol of this created life we have in Christ — and of our Advent/Christmas season, too — may be found in this branch from a tree ... an evergreen. We use "evergreen" as a name for a certain type of shrub or bush or tree. Evergreen. But evergreen is also what it is. It is ever green. We know that this type of tree is a symbol of life, for it never loses its needles or leaves in winter. Rather, this tree remains green — *ever* green — all year long. It is always filled with life, continually reminding us of the life — the gift of life here and eternally — that is ours in Jesus Christ.

Green is the color of life, but the color green can also have some negative connotations. When I mention the color green to you, what is the first thing that pops into your head? Do you think of Christmas trees, evergreens, the green leaves, plants, and grass of a summer day? Or, do you think of something else that is green, something else that has replaced God in the minds of many, many people? I'm referring, of course, to the "idol" money! The love of money is referred to in the Bible as the root of all evil. Indeed, Paul told his brother, Timothy, that very truth. And it can be true for us, too, if we let money become the "idol" of our lives, that which we worship above all else. But this green money has another side to it, too. Money can be a positive, powerful force in doing God's will, in helping others, if we will but use it properly. It's a fact: We cannot live in this world today without money. But, we can do a lot of good with it. It's not meant to be hoarded, but invested for God's greater glory. We are but stewards of God's many and varied gifts.

During the announcements this morning, and in your Sunday bulletin, too, we heard and read about a local Christmas Cheer program.* This program offers you and me a joyous way of sharing the blessings of God with others. Green money is needed and you can help. Likewise, on your Sunday envelope, there are many wonderful programs supported by our green dollars. Our own congregation depends upon our green money to continue to do the work we do. Money, when used properly, is an important tool, a life-giving tool for Christians, at Christmas time and all year long. But, if it becomes our god, then, my friends, we're in real trouble. Then the love of money becomes the root of all evil. As responsible Christians, we need to make responsible decisions.

In chapter 23 of John's Gospel, Jesus, himself, spoke of the color green. Jesus referred to it as he was being led on his way to Golgotha, to be nailed to the wooden cross and put to death. As he was going, the women of Jerusalem came weeping and wailing after Jesus. Jesus told the women that they should not weep for him, but for themselves and their children. For the days are coming, says the Lord, when Jerusalem itself will be destroyed. And it is then that we encounter these strangely prophetic words: "For if they do this when the wood is green, what will happen when it is dry?"

Jesus said that the wood was green in those former days, but many believe today that the wood is very, very dry ... that the end is near, and it is in this context that we gather today. We gather to celebrate the beginning once more of Advent, looking for the Babe of Bethlehem and the Christ of glory who promises to come once more.

There is a beautiful relationship here, then, between the life we have on this earth, this place, and the hope of eternal life that is ours in Christ. We know that both "lives" are gifts from our Lord. This color, green, reminds us of life ... and the life God has given us ... the life we live in his love and forgiveness.

I pray that this holiday season might be for each of us a season of life, a season of green. May we find in our preparation, our anticipation, and our celebration that intangible something from God that makes this life — all life — really worth the living! Have a blessed, green, life-filled holiday season, in Jesus Christ, our Lord. Amen.

----

*Churches can insert any local "giving" program.

Purple Or Violet

Good morning, boys and girls. I'm happy to see so many of you wearing your green ribbons this morning. See, I have mine, too. What does the color green remind us of? That's right, life and growth. Very good. Yes, God has given us all things in creation, including his Son, Jesus. Green reminds us of the life we have in his love, and is certainly a good color for the Christmas season. Just look at the beautiful green Christmas tree today!

We have a new color this morning, another color of Christmas. What color did I mention during my announcements? That's right. *Purple* or *violet*. And here, I have a purple ribbon for each of you to wear. This morning, a few of the women from our choir are going to help you pin your ribbons on while I tell you about purple or violet.

Why is purple a good color for Christmas? Any ideas? This may be a bit more difficult to understand for us, since purple isn't common for the Christmas season, is it? Purple is the color of royalty. Kings and princes often wear purple robes as a symbol of their authority and power. Who is the great King of kings, whose birthday we're preparing to celebrate? That's right, Jesus. So, because Jesus is our great king, purple is a wonderful color for Christmas.

Do you see anything that is violet or purple in the sanctuary this morning? That's right, the altar cloths or paraments. Anything else? Very good, the candles on the Advent wreath. They are purple ... the candles for the king. Anything else? Well, there is one more place, but you can't see it from here. Purple is also the color of grapes, and what do many people make out of grapes? Wine (Juice)? Yes, wine (juice). This morning, we will celebrate Holy Communion, the coming of the king, the coming of Jesus to each of us in a special way. We celebrate this Lord's Supper with bread and wine (juice), prepared and waiting for us on the altar.

Purple or violet. It reminds us of what? That's right, that Jesus is the King of kings. Other kings came seeking Jesus, too. We call them the Wise Men. All in all, purple is a great color of Christmas.

Purple Or Violet, The Color Of Royalty

Luke 1:31-35; 23:33-38

"Prepare the royal highway ... the King of kings is near!" This is Advent! Together, as God's people in Jesus Christ, we look for the coming of our Lord. Last Sunday morning, we began our celebration of the Advent/Christmas season with a look at the colors of Christmas! For our first color, our emphasis last Sunday was on green, the color of life. We spoke of Christ Jesus, the Babe of Bethlehem, as the source of all life, both life in this world and life for all believers in the next. Today, we look at purple or violet, the color of royalty. It is the color of kings, and especially the King of kings whose birth is certainly drawing near!

As a prelude to our consideration this morning, I'd like to share with you two portions of God's Word, from the Gospel of Luke. First, Luke 1:31-35 and then Luke 23:33-38.

From the beginning of Luke's Gospel, until the very end of it, we find Jesus, our Lord, called king. The angel announced it at his conception and birth. The Jews, on the other hand, sarcastically proclaimed Jesus as king of the Jews as he died on the cross for the sins of all the world. Jesus, the king ... the royal son of David. In birth and in death, he is called king. "Prepare the royal highway ... the King of kings is here!"

A royal king, standing in the line of David, was exactly what the Jews were looking for when Jesus was born. The society of Israel to which Jesus came was a society filled with oppression. Rome was in absolute control. They exacted tribute from their Jewish subjects. No one dared oppose their rule. A few had tried, and most of them had paid the ultimate price. The Jews longed for a new prince, a new king, a new anointed one, a messiah like David to restore Judah to its lofty place of political prominence.

48

History is very important to the Jewish people. Following the death of David and Solomon, and with the assumption of the throne by King Rehoboam, the nation of Israel had suffered from internal strife and continual decline. No king was remembered more fondly than King David. So, remember him they did, for it was David who had consolidated the territory of Israel and expanded the nation. It was David who had established Jersualem as Israel's capital. It was David who had won many great victories over Israel's enemies, and it was David who had founded a dynasty of kings. And so it was David who was remembered reverently, hopefully. Wouldn't it be great if we could just have another king like David? If only King David would return and throw the Romans out! The prophets fueled this longing for another David through the continual promises of God.

For example, in our first lesson for this morning, Isaiah calls for a shoot, a branch from the stump of Jesse. You remember Jesse, David's father. Likewise, our psalm for the day is a psalm of Solomon. It is actually a prayer of blessing for a righteous king.

Though their powerful nation was gone ... though kings like David no longer existed, still the Jews remembered ... they remembered King David and longed for such royalty once more.

It was into this world of remembering and anticipation that Jesus came. The angel called him king. The Wise Men recognized him in the same way: "Where is he who has been born king of the Jews?" But in reality, Jesus was just the opposite of the great king and military leader the people were hoping for. The Jews expected power, authority, military victories, and revolt. Instead, Jesus came filled with "the spirit of wisdom and understanding, the spirit of council and justice, the spirit of knowledge, and the fear of the Lord!" (Isaiah 11:2).

And it was Isaiah's prophecy that came true in the life and teachings of Jesus of Nazareth. He fulfilled all that was spoken about him concerning the prophets. But the Jews ... ah, well, the Jews! They just didn't know what to make of this Jesus. They missed the royal king when he came knocking on their doors. Only at Jesus' death, did they call him king ... king of the Jews, but this was simply a cruel, humorless joke.

In retrospect, how can we blame them? Given their political situation and their longings for a king, how can we blame them? Did Jesus look like a king? Did he act like a king? How was Jesus dressed? Did he wear the purple robe of a king?

Actually, he *did* wear a purple robe once in his life. Mark's Gospel reports that as Jesus was taken as a prisoner to the palace, the soldiers clothed Jesus in a purple cloak, and plaiting a crown of thorns, they put it on him. They began to salute him, "Hail, king of the Jews!" They struck him with a reed and spit upon him, and they knelt down in mock homage to him. And after they mocked him, they stripped him of the purple cloak, they put his own clothes on him, and they led him out to be crucified.

Purple or violet is the color of royalty. It is reserved for kings' palaces, not mangers and stables. Yet purple or violet is a color of Christmas. It is the color we generally see hanging from the altar, lectern, pulpit, and pastor during Advent. It is the color we use during the Lenten season, too, since it is also a color of repentance.

The color purple or violet, Christ the king, and repentance have a lot in common. Our sins have been confessed this morning. We know that because of Christ, our king's loving death for our sakes, our sins have been eliminated; washed away. This king, our king, our royal king Jesus, sacrificed himself for his subjects. He took off the purple robe in heaven, and put on the diapers of Bethlehem for our sakes. He took off the purple robe in Herod's palace, willingly laying down his life on the cross for our sakes.

The color for today, this color of Christmas, is purple or violet. We use it and we wear it, so that we may never, ever forget what he has done for us all.

In another way, remembering will be part of our worship this morning, too. On the evening before Jesus died, he took a cup of wine — wine made from purple grapes just like these — and mysteriously, miraculously, changed the eating habits of Christians forever. For as we gather here, Advent comes true ... the king comes to us once more, through his own body, his own blood. We celebrate, we rejoice, we remember, we repent!

"Prepare the royal highway ... the King of kings is near!" Purple or violet is the color of royalty! As you gather during this holiday season with family and friends, may you remember whose birthday we are celebrating. May you remember the angel's message, "For to you is born this day in the city of David, a Savior, a Messiah, who is Christ the Lord!" That babe born in Bethlehem, so very long ago, is Christ the king ... your king ... my king!

Purple or violet is the color of royalty. "Then greet the king of glory, foretold in sacred story. Hosanna to the Lord ... for he fulfills God's Word!" Amen.

Red

Good morning, boys and girls. I'm pleased to see each of you wearing your ribbons this morning. Let's go over them together. The green ribbon reminds us of life and growth, doesn't it? And the purple one? That's correct, it reminds us that Jesus is the King of kings! Very good. Notice that I'm wearing my green and purple ribbons this morning, too!

Well, this morning's color certainly fits the Christmas season, doesn't it? What color is it? That's right, it's *red*. Red is probably the best known color of the Christmas season. Can you name some things that are red that we often associate with Christmas? Santa Claus. Yes, that's a good answer. Santa's suit is bright red, isn't it? Rudolph's nose? That's another good answer. Many of the Christmas presents under the Christmas tree are red, too, aren't they? Red ribbons and bows, red wrapping paper, candy canes ... those are all good answers.

Well, this morning I want to tell you about a few more items that make red such an excellent color for Christmas. Here are your red ribbons and one for me, too. Let's ask the women of the choir to help you again as I talk about red as a color of Christmas.

Red is the color of blood, of sacrifice. If you would cut your finger, even just a little bit, what would come out of the cut? That's right, blood. And what color is blood? Yes, it's red — bright red. Christmas is the celebration of the birth of God's Son, Jesus. Jesus came to this earth to live, and to die. Jesus died on the cross to save us from our sins. He sacrificed himself, gave his blood, that we might belong to God forever. So with red, we remember to celebrate Christmas, and what it means for God to love us enough that he would sacrifice, give up his own Son. Red is a good color of Christmas. It means a lot more than just Santa Claus, presents, and candy canes, though, doesn't it? It reminds us that Jesus died on the cross to save us all!

Red, The Color Of Sacrifice

Genesis 22:1-14; Matthew 2:16-18

Of all the colors of Christmas, I suppose red is the most prominent. Look around you, in our beautiful sanctuary this morning. We see red bows, red lights, red paper — even the paraments, the cross around my neck, and the ribbons I gave the youngsters today are red. But, there is more of a meaning to the "red" of Christmas than all of these red things that surround us today.

Just as the green spoke to us of life two weeks ago, and purple or violet suggested the royalty of Christ last Sunday, today red has a special meaning, too. I alluded to it with the youngsters, but I want to take it one step further with all of you. God's Word sheds some light on this meaning of sacrifice, and I'd like to look at fourteen verses of Genesis 22, followed by just three verses, verses 16-18 of Matthew 2.

(Read the text.)

In the Genesis story I just read, we see old Abraham now well past 100 years of age, willing to sacrifice his young, probably teenage son, just because the Lord God told him it was the thing to do.

Isaac meant a lot to his father, Abraham. And no wonder. Abraham and Sarah had tried for years and years to have a son. But, Sarah just never became pregnant. There were no great medical specialists in those days, so Abraham and Sarah had contented themselves with the knowledge that for some reason, they would not have a son, an heir.

Then God entered the picture. He made a promise, an agreement, a covenant with Abraham. He told Abraham that he would be the father of a great nation. That the descendants of their family would be as the sands of the sea. Sarah laughed when she heard about God's promise. But, even at age ninety, God could still work a miracle in this laughing wife of Abraham. And he did. Isaac was born and they believed the promise of God. There was more than just a great nation connected to the promise. God had said that, through their descendants, one would come to set right all that had gone wrong. A Messiah, a Savior was the promise.

But now all of that was in jeopardy as Isaac and Abraham climbed the mountain: sacrifice his own son, tie him to the altar and kill him with a knife? That had been the command of God and Abraham sought to obey. It looked as if the promise would be lost in the red blood of Isaac, slain as a sacrifice to God. First the altar, then the wood, then the ropes, then the knife. And suddenly, as the knife was drawn forth, the hand of God intervened. It had been a test, a test of faith, and so the son, the heir, was saved. The blood was not shed.

This is a remarkable story, filled with so much of Christmas. God willingly sent his own Son to earth, and laid him in the manger at Bethlehem. God the Father knew that it meant real sacrifice, that indeed, the red blood of Jesus must be shed for the sins of the world. Like Abraham, God did not withhold his Son of promise, but willingly gave him up for the sins of humankind.

In the second reading, we find that this baby Jesus has been spared. The Wise Men had been warned not to return to Herod, so they didn't. Instead, they departed for their homeland by another way. Herod, realizing that he had been tricked by the Wise Men, decided to do away with Jesus himself. He sent his soldiers to Bethlehem, and the slaughter was underway. Herod sacrificed the blood of hundreds of youngsters for his own selfish gain. Again, just as at the cross, red blood was shed and weeping was heard!

Both stories deal with sacrifice, and give us a prelude to the events of Good Friday. I guess whether we like to think about it or not, Jesus was born into this world to die. He came to Bethlehem as a baby, but the road would lead to Calvary and his own death. "Come thou long-expected Jesus, born to set thy people free!"

It's interesting to note that in reality we know precious little about the birth of Christ. John and Mark do not mention it at all. Matthew has a scant seven verses dealing with Jesus' birth. The rest we learn from Saint Luke and that is only some twenty verses. No, the birth of Jesus has its importance only as a prelude to the death and resurrection of our Lord. It is in looking back at Jesus' sacrifice for the sins of the world, that his birth, his incarnation take on majestic meaning!

Lest we spend all of our time with long faces this third Sunday of Advent, let us remember that red is also the color of celebration and rejoicing. Red shines about us at Christmas ... in packages shared, in candy canes consumed, in Santa's red suit, in the glow of children's faces! Red is the color of celebration and joy. The same is true in the church. We use red for our festival holidays: reformation, confirmation, ordination, and we also use red to celebrate the church's birthday, the festival of Pentecost! Red truly is a color of Christmas, fitting both in the home and in the church. For just as we use it to celebrate the church's birthday, we should use it to celebrate Christ's birthday. The two are inseparably linked together.

Christmas Day is two weeks away. Red poinsettias will adorn the sanctuary. We will celebrate the birth of Jesus, but as we celebrate, as we worship, as we gather with our families around the altar and the colorful Christmas tree, let us remember that our Lord Jesus came joyously, courageously, at Christmas, came as the perfect Lamb of God, the sacrifice for all of our sins.

Sacrifice is a tough word for us. It's difficult to understand. We have so much in life ... and we are asked to give so little. God gave everything he had, the greatest Christmas gift ever, that the red blood of Jesus Christ might cleanse us forever, bringing us back into the perfect relationship with him.

One good way for us to remember this red sacrifice might be through the love God has given us. The heart, like the heart of a giant, red Valentine, is the center of such love, and God gives his very heart to us at Christmas. May its red glow, and may all the red of Christmas, remind us of that love, that celebration, that sacrifice for us — in the name of Christ, our Lord! Amen.

Blue

Good morning, boys and girls. What color ribbons do we have this morning? *Blue.* Yes, we have blue ribbons today. Blue is our color of Christmas for this morning. But, before we pass out the blue ribbons and talk about them, let's review the three we already have. First, we had green. The green ribbon stands for what? Correct, life and growth. Next, we had the purple ribbon. It reminds us that Jesus is the King of kings. Last Sunday's ribbon was red. Through the color red, we remember that Jesus died on the cross to save us all.

And now the blue ribbons. Once again, the women of the choir will help you pin on your blue ribbons while I talk to you about the color blue as a color of Christmas.

This morning, the altar paraments are blue in color, just like our ribbons. Blue. When a new baby is born, and the baby happens to be a little girl, in what color is she often dressed? Pink, that's correct. What color is used if the baby is a boy? That's right, blue. Blue seems to be the color for boys, doesn't it? But, there's more behind the color blue than the fact that Jesus was a baby boy. Blue is also the color of heaven or eternity. What color is the sky on a bright and sunny day? That's correct, it's blue. Likewise, when we think of water, what color comes to mind? Blue again. And what do we use water for in the church? Baptism, that's right. When most of you were little babies, you were brought here to the altar and baptized. The pastor took water and poured it over your head, so that you might become a child of God. During the Christmas season, we remember once more the coming of the Child of God, Jesus. He came down to us from heaven. He was baptized by John the Baptist in the Jordan River. He is God's Son and our Savior for eternity.

As you can see, there are several good reasons that blue is one of the colors of Christmas. Wear your blue ribbon proudly. It reminds us of the baby boy born in Bethlehem, Jesus, our eternal Savior! And through the color blue, we can remember our baptism also as a child of God!

Blue, The Color Of Eternity

Romans 6:3-11

I once heard of a dream about Christmas. It's not the usual dream of a baby boy in the manger in the stable at Bethlehem. Rather, the dream goes something like this:

One day, our Lord Jesus entered the office of the angel in charge of foreign relations in heaven. "I just heard that I might be making a trip down to earth...." The angel allowed his gold pencil two taps on his desk. "That's right ... and soon, too." "Well," continues Jesus, "what I want to know is where? Where on earth? Rome? Athens? Corinth? Alexandria? There's a fine library in Alexandria, and I hear that the emperor's symphony at Rome is even better than the Athens Philharmonic, and I would love to see the Parthenon in person, too...." His voice trailed off.

Without speaking, the angel got up and went over to the large map on the wall. He took his pencil and found the Mediterranean Sea; he touched Rome. Jesus' heart stopped for a moment ... then moved east to Corinth and Athens ... the Lord held his breath. The pencil continued to move east, then south. The angel seemed to be having a little trouble finding the place he was looking for. Then he spotted Jerusalem; holding the pencil point on Jerusalem, he looked around it in a small circle. "I guess it's just too little to be on the map." "Too little? What's too little?" the Lord asked. "Bethlehem," was the answer.

"Bethlehem!" The Lord's jaw dropped. "You mean I'm going to Bethlehem?" The angel didn't deny it. "But ... but there's nothing there, nothing at all. No symphonies, no libraries, no works of art, no centers of learning. There won't even be decent living accommodations ... just a little rundown inn! How can I set up my office there?"

The angel cleared his throat and tried to find just the right words. "We weren't thinking of having you set up an office. You'll be going steerage this trip."

"Steerage! No office — Bethlehem! I had hoped for something a little better than Bethlehem. Well, I might as well start packing."

At this point, the angel put his hand on the Lord's shoulder. "Ummm, that won't be necessary! I don't know how to tell you this, but we're sending you in the same way all humans enter the world ... we're sending you as a baby."

There was a long, long silence. "As a baby! As a *baby*? Are you sure? Why, there isn't even a decent hospital in Bethlehem!"

"I know, I know," said the angel gently. "You'll just have to make the best of things."

Slowly, the Lord walked out of the angel's office, mumbling to himself, "To Bethlehem — not to Rome, or Corinth, or Athens. Bethlehem? To a dingy, dirty, out-of-the way place like Bethlehem ... and going as a baby on top of it all! Bethlehem, of all places! With my luck, the inn will probably be full up when I arrive!"

At Christmas, Jesus came to earth as a baby boy! The mighty Son of God — the Lord of all nations — the Prince of Peace! A baby — a little baby boy. And we know that the color blue is the color of baby boys!

But, like the green, the purple, and the red that have preceded it, blue has a deeper meaning as well. It is also the color of eternity. It reminds us of heaven, of the place where we are going in order to be with God, the place from where Jesus came in the first place! Eternity — a relationship we have with this little baby boy of Bethlehem. It's a relationship that is borne out, that begins with baptism. Listen with me to the words of Saint Paul from Romans, chapter 6.

(Read the text.)

Alive to God in Christ Jesus! Doesn't sound much like the Christmas story, does it? More like Easter? Exactly! And that's the point. This baby boy, dressed in blue as a color of Christmas, is the same victorious Christ of Easter. And the victory, the glory, the

59

hope and promise of eternity is ours, through the blue water of baptism!

My little "dream" about Jesus descending to earth as a child, I believe, points out vividly to what great lengths God our Father went to save us, his children. His only begotten Son, reduced to a mere infant, a baby boy, the child of Bethlehem.

Matthew tells the story of the angel's appearance to Joseph. What a conversation Joseph and Mary must have had the night before! "You're what? Pregnant? What a disgrace! You're nothing but a harlot! You've ruined my reputation and your own!"

But the angel comes with these words: "Joseph, do not fear to take Mary your wife, for that which is conceived in her is of the Holy Spirit; she will bear a son, and you shall call his name Jesus, for he will save his people from their sins!" So the gift God gave the world at Christmas was the greatest gift he could possibly give. His own Son, his own little boy, the Child who comes to give us the gift of eternity!

A December issue of *Readers' Digest* from many years ago had this little story that shares with us much of the truth of Christmas:

> *There was once an African boy who gave his mission-*
> *ary teacher an exquisite sea shell as a Christmas gift.*
> *The lad had walked miles and miles for it, to a special*
> *bay, the only place where such sea shells were found.*
> *"How wonderful of you to have traveled so far for this*
> *present," said the teacher. The boy's eyes shone as he*
> *replied, "Long walk, part of gift!"*

It was a long walk from Nazareth to Bethlehem, from eternity to Bethlehem, but the long walk was part of God's gift ... that we might know eternity ... that we might experience life as God in-tended ... that we might be with him forever!

Blue, the color of eternity. One of the colors of Christmas. Think about your baptism and God's gift to you of the baby boy at Bethlehem, as you celebrate your Christmas in a few short days. Because of the Christ of Christmas, we have the gift of eternity. Enjoy your gift, your Christmas gift from God, this Christmas. Joy to the world, the Lord has come! Amen.

Christmas Eve/Day
Children's Message

White

Good evening, boys and girls. Merry Christmas to each of you. Tonight, I have another ribbon for each of you. It's a special ribbon, tonight, and a special color, the color *white*. It's good to see many of you wearing your four, colored ribbons this evening. I have my four ribbons, too. Together, let's review the colors. The green one stands for life and growth. That's what Jesus gives each of us. The purple one reminds us that Jesus is — what? The King of kings, that's right. And the red one? It helps us remember that Jesus died on the cross to save us from our sins. Last Sunday, I gave you your blue ribbon. The blue one reminds us of many things. We think of heaven, the blue sky, the baby boy, Jesus, and also our baptism. Well, each of these ribbons has been but a prelude to the ribbon I'm giving you this evening. Let's ask the women of the choir to help you pin them on, as I share with you once more the story of Christmas.

Tonight and tomorrow, we celebrate the birth of Jesus. How many of you remember when you were born? We can't remember back that far, can we? But, how many of you have younger brothers or sisters? Okay. Do you recall how excited everyone was when they were born? Your parents were just as happy, just as thrilled when you were born! And you can imagine then, all the joy in earth and heaven when Jesus was born! The angels came from heaven to sing at Jesus' birth. The shepherds left their sheep to come and see this special Child of God. Mary wrapped Jesus in some cloths and probably put something that looks like this on Jesus. What is it? That's right, a diaper. Do you see why white is the perfect color for Christmas? Angels, sheep, diapers, but there's even more. White is the color of purity and holiness. It represents Jesus as the spotless Lamb of God. White also reminds us of the fluffy, white snow that blankets the ground almost every

Christmas. It's as though God's purifying the whole earth through the coming of his holy Son, Jesus.

I'm sure you're excited about Christmas. I am, too. We all are. But, during all of the excitement, let's remember the purity, the holiness, the color of this season — white. Jesus is the perfect Son of God. Let's celebrate his birthday together, singing his praises, just like the angels. We have one more color of Christmas, and I'll share that with you this Sunday. I'll see you then. Have a Merry Christmas!

White, The Color
Of Purity And Holiness

Luke 2:1-20

Yesterday morning, amid the cold, the snow, and the blowing wind, I ventured down to the church to work on this Christmas message. I made two stops on the way — one at the gas station to top off my gas tank. There I saw several cars being jumped, pushed, coaxed, and begged into running. I was very thankful that my key brought the engine to life. My other stop was at the grocery store to pick up a gallon of milk. The store was busy, crowded with people picking up those last-minute necessities for Christmas, and of course, just in case the weather worsened and we were all snowed in.

As I stood in line at the checkout, an older gentleman was talking to a friend. They were discussing the terrible weather, and the younger one remarked that this certainly had to be the worst Christmas weather he could remember. Well, such a remark, directed at the older gentleman, was bound to elicit the remark. "Well, I can remember a Christmas with weather even worse than this. When I was a boy, we had a Christmas even worse than this. We had a Christmas with a temperature of eighteen degrees below zero and six feet of snow. The wind was blowing and drifting the snow." He went on to describe a bitter, cold day, but one on which warmth and love was shared among family and friends.

This conversation prompted several thoughts in my mind as I considered this Christmas festival. First of all, though the weather outside is frightful, inside, with all of you, it's so delightful! Today, with our modern ways of heating our homes, our cars, our churches, we can live in relative comfort in spite of the weather. We have learned how to conquer, if not control, the environment. This Christmas, even if it is one of the coldest ever, can be one of the warmest because of the conveniences of our modern world. We are warm and comfortable in here (and those who could not get to church this morning need only listen to their radio and we will bring the Christmas Day service of St. Martin's Lutheran Church right into their homes).* The "good old days" have a lot of fond memories for many, but on a day like today, I'm thankful for our technological achievements. Thank you, good Lord!

Secondly, we've often heard the phrase, "Christmas is for children!" In many ways, that does seem true enough. Most of our best memories of Christmas are of those special Christmases when we were children. The beautiful gifts, the magnificent Christmas tree, those great "goodies" to eat, and that part we all had to memorize for the Sunday church school Christmas program are the things that pop into our heads when we think of Christmas. Those special times live again, anew each year as we decorate, wrap, and prepare ourselves for the holiday season. The Christmas of today will be for some of us, especially the youngsters, the glorious memory of Christmas tomorrow. Someday, when they are as old and wise as we adults, they will remark, "Why I remember a Christmas when it was bitter cold; few were able to get out, to come and worship; yet, it was perhaps the best Christmas ever!"

Finally, the third idea that popped into my mind is this: Where must we all be today? It's in Bethlehem, on another cold, winter day, when Mary, God's chosen handmaiden, gave birth to her first-born son, wrapped him in swaddling cloths, and laid him in a manger. Listen again, with me, to that old, old story of the greatest Christmas ever, Luke 2:1-20.

(Read the text.)

Christmas is Jesus' birthday. On Christmas, God touched the earth with his love, his forgiveness, his peace, his purity, and his holiness for all people. The color white is certainly that color. White snow, the white glow of candlelight on a child's face, the whiteness of angels' wings as they share good news of a great joy, the whiteness of the Lamb of God who comes to take away the sin of the world, the whiteness of a newborn baby's diaper. Purity and holiness in Christ our Lord.

Perhaps the man was right. Christmas *is* for children, for it was as a child that Jesus came and he tells us that we must come with childlike faith to understand his love and receive his blessing. And don't we all become children again at Christmas? Aren't we innocent and pure once more, looking forward and yet looking back to Christmases long ago — and to the first Christmas long, long ago? In the spirit of God's love and the truth of Christmas, I'd like to close with the words of a simple Christmas poem, a special poem for this special day:

The Stable
In that little stable so long ago
There were no dazzling lights.
There was nothing to distract one's thoughts
From that precious, holy sight.

High above, the brilliant star
Was shining down from heaven.
And in the stillness of that moment
God's wondrous gift was given.

Shepherds came from near and far
Their hearts were filled with love
And watching o'er the little child
Were angels from above.

The three Wise Men bearing gifts
At last on him did gaze,
And as they looked in wonderment
Their lips were uttering praise.

So take a moment to recall
How this season did begin,
And make your heart a quiet stable
Where the Lord may enter in.

— Unknown

May the peace, joy, the holiness and purity that is Christmas be yours, giving you comfort and confidence, for the new year! Merry Christmas, my friends!

Amen.

---

*Adapt for local use.

Christmas 1
Children's Message

Gold

Good morning, boys and girls. It's good to see all of you here.
Did you have a Merry Christmas? That's great! Wow! Look at all
of those ribbons you're wearing this morning. How many do you
have? That's right! We each have five ribbons. A green one that
stands for life and growth; a purple one that stands for Jesus, the
King of kings; a red one that reminds us of the sacrifice Jesus has
made for us; a blue one that teaches us that Jesus, God's Son, came
down from heaven; and a white one that represents the perfect Son
of God, Jesus our Savior.

Today, you will receive your last ribbon from me. What color
is it? *Gold.* Aren't these gold ribbons pretty? They look great with
the others. Gold is the color of wealth and riches. When someone
has something gold colored, we think of it as being expensive, worth
a great deal of money. Gold was one of the gifts brought to Jesus
by ... whom? The Wise Men, that's correct. The Wise Men brought
great treasures to Jesus, gifts of gold, frankincense, and myrrh.
Gold also represents the Star of Bethlehem that guided the Wise
Men as they searched for Jesus. Finally, the straw of the manger is
gold in color. Though Jesus is the greatest king ever, his birth was
lowly and humble, born in a stable behind the Bethlehem inn.

The colors of Christmas — you have them represented by ribbons: green, purple, red, blue, white, and gold. I hope you'll keep
your ribbons and that each Christmas they may remind you of all
we've learned about Christ Jesus and Christmas this year. Thanks
for sharing in this special time with me as we've talked about the
colors of Christmas together. Let's celebrate the truth of Christmas
each day throughout this coming year. God bless you all!

Gold, The Color Of Wealth And Riches

Matthew 2:1-12

As we face a new year, it is customary in America to greet one another with the phrase, "Happy New Year!"

But, New Year's Day may not be that happy for some. On New Year's morning, many, many people across our land are not happy with their headaches and hangovers because of the previous evening's excessive dining, drinking, and dancing. And, how can we be happy if the new year is just more of the same old things — the same poverty, unemployment, inflation, terrorism, sickness, war, and failure? When we reflect upon things even just briefly, we certainly have cause to ask the question, "Just what's so great, what's 'happy' about the new year?"

Now, lest we bury our heads in our hands and give up, even before the new year has begun, let's consider what happened last week. You know, Christmas! You remember Christmas, don't you? It was in all the papers. It's the biggest holiday of the year. There's a Christmas tree, lots of presents, Santa Claus comes, it falls on December 25. Ah, yes, you remember about Christmas, don't you?

But, there is more, much more to Christmas than all that stuff and that's what makes the new year happy. "For to you is born in the city of David a Savior who is Christ the Lord!" God has come to show us how to live, how to live together in joy, hope, and peace for all people. He came at Christmas to make a difference in peoples' lives — in your life and mine.

One thing is sure: the coming of Jesus as the Babe of Bethlehem certainly made the difference in the lives of those Wise Men from the East. They traveled many, many miles just to offer gifts to the newborn king of the Jews. Let's listen to their story as Matthew tells it in Matthew 2:1-12.

(Read the text.)

And they offered him gifts of gold, frankincense, and myrrh. When we think of gold, we think of riches, wealth, and power. And it is certainly that. In our world, in this society, the person with gold — with money — has wealth, riches, and power. But gold is also a color. Consider the beautiful gold ribbons I gave the children this morning. Gold is bright, the color of sunlight and starlight, the color of straw, all of these reminding us of our Lord's most humble birth.

Isn't the coming of the Christ of Christmas the real wealth of the season, the riches of a new year that is just beginning? It is the love of God, Jesus Christ, our Lord!

Those Wise Men were rich. They came bringing with them gifts, treasures fit for a king. The gifts represented much wealth. Yet, when the Magi saw this little baby poor and humble, in the arms of his mother, a simple, young maiden, they fell down and worshiped him. They recognized that in this child, the earth had been blessed in a special way by God. So they humbled themselves, offered their greatest treasures, knelt and gave homage to Jesus.

And when this same Jesus grew up, he taught people about riches and how they are to be used. "Do not lay up for yourselves treasures on earth, where moth and rust consume and where thieves break in and steal, but lay up for yourselves treasures in heaven, where neither moth nor rust consumes and where thieves do not break in and steal. For where your treasure is, there will your heart be, also."

Here our Lord is not speaking of saving money. He's speaking instead of saving souls. Money, riches, wealth, power, and gold are not to become our idols, our gods that we put above God. We must be willing to give it up. We are to be Christians, believers in Christ and his love first and foremost.

Some time ago, a man handed me a card with the question on it, "If you were arrested for being a Christian, would there be enough evidence to convict you?" That makes me stop and think. Are we Christians in our day-to-day living? Are we putting our treasures in heaven? Are we taking a stand against evil for the right, or are

69

we compromising so well with the world that it is impossible to tell a Christian from a non-Christian?

We can become too "relevant to the world," so that we forget who we are. We lose our distinctiveness as Christians. There was once a man who loved the color yellow. He had yellow carpet in his home. He also had yellow drapes, yellow furniture, a yellow bedspread, and yellow pajamas. But, one day he became very sick. He contracted yellow jaundice. His wife sent for the doctor who went right to his home to examine him. His wife showed the doctor into the man's bedroom. Shortly, the doctor came out of the room. The wife asked immediately how her husband was doing. The physician replied, "How's he doing? I don't know. I couldn't find him!"

We, likewise, must be careful, watchful, that we do not become lost in the worldly ways of our age. Like the Wise Men of old, we must learn to give our gifts, our gold, away if it is to accomplish the purpose for which God intended. Gifts are, after all, only gifts *when they are given to someone else.*

Our last color of the Christmas season is gold. As we face the new year, may we learn the golden lesson the Wise Men shared, that to be happy and at peace in this world, we must place our God first, above all things, all gifts, all gold. It is in doing this that we will understand what wealth is.

As you begin the new year, as you join with me here at our Lord's Table, may you receive the most precious gift God offers you this holiday season — himself. May you find a wealth of happiness and joy in his great love for you. Have a happy, blessed, peaceful, and joyful new year. My friends, Happy New Year! Amen.

Is This The Road To Bethlehem?

A Children's Liturgy For Advent

Judy Gattis Smith

Introduction

Deep inside every person is a basic need to celebrate, to worship. This need is present from the very beginning of our lives.

Children are a part of the worshiping community, but are often left out of the service. Our services of worship, Sunday after Sunday, are geared specifically to adults. The words, both written and spoken, the movements, and the symbols are often foreign to a child's understanding. Children should have the experience of meeting God as well as learning and studying about God. Worship should not be put off until they can understand and identify with adult liturgy.

Contained in the following pages is a service written specifically for children's worship. Other age levels are welcome and encouraged to join the worship experience, but the focus is on the interests and expressions of children. The elements that we associate with worship are present: praise of God, prayers for forgiveness, affirmation of faith, dedication of lives, but the form may seem strange.

"The Spirit blows where it will" and no one can guarantee when the divine presence will break through in a human situation. These liturgies are based on the belief and expectation that God will come to all his children, even the young ones, if we sincerely prepare and await his presence.

The belief is inherent in this liturgy that God loves children as they are and, if they turn to him, there he is in their midst, laughing and celebrating with them, drying their small tears and enlarging their world of pets and school and family with his presence.

Let the children come — and worship God.

Preparation For The Service

Christmas is one of the great festival times in the church year. This service attempts to show children that this event followed a period of long waiting: that Christmas was not just an event in Bethlehem, but was the culmination of peoples' hopes and dreams.

Preparations

1. Choose a child leader for the responsive sentences and prayer.

2. Arrange with the children's choir or a church school class for special music.

3. Cut out wooden figures and stands for action/sermon. Have the children paint them as per instructions. Posterboard may be substituted for wood.

4. Choose six children to take part in the action/sermon. Practice.

5. Check with the church school classes about the presentation of gifts (preschool children with mittens; elementary classes with small toys; older elementary classes with food). Perhaps you would prefer other gifts and other recipients. Perhaps it would be good to use local charities and recipients.

6. Practice with the acolytes for the ritual of lighting the Advent candles.

Wooden Figures

Cut from 1/2-inch plywood, six figures, approximately 14 inches tall.

Paint with a prime coat of white. Let dry. Draw features and paint robes with tempera or oil paints.

Cut pieces of wood for stand. Groove each so that characters feet fit and they stand.

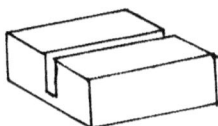

Note: If wooden figures cannot be made, use heavy posterboard and follow the same pattern. Weight the lower portion so the figures will stand.

Props

You will need a long table with an appropriately sized manger at one end. This table is used to display the wooden or posterboard figures and is, in essence, the "road to Bethlehem."

Order Of Service

Prelude

Welcome

Procession Of Acolytes

Opening Hymn: "O Come, Little Children"

Responsive Sentences

Prayer

Scripture

Children's Choir Anthem

Action/Sermon

Presentation Of Gifts

Closing Hymn: "O Come, All Ye Faithful"

Script

Prelude

Welcome

Leader: Welcome to our children's liturgy. We come together today to think about and celebrate the birth of Jesus.

Procession Of Acolytes
(Acolytes enter down aisle as Leader reads)

Leader: Men travel bravely by 1,000 roads
　　Some broad and lined with palaces
　　Some hard and steep and lonely which blindly twist through tangled jungles where there is no light.
　　And mostly they are traveled thoughtlessly;
　　But once a year an ancient question comes to every traveler passing on the way.
　　A question that can stab and burn, or bless,
　　"Is this the road that leads to Bethlehem?"
　　　　　　　　　　　　　　　　— Source Unknown

Leader: Let the candles that light that path be lighted.

(Acolytes light Advent candles)

Opening Hymn　　　　　　　　"O Come, Little Children"

Responsive Sentences
Child Leader:　We come thankfully before you, O God;
Response:　**On the road to Bethlehem.**
Child Leader:　We join with the Wise Men who bring great gifts;
Response:　**On the road to Bethlehem.**

78

Child Leader:	We join the lowly shepherds who hurry to the stable;
Response:	**On the road to Bethlehem.**
Child Leader:	We join with our family, our friends, and our church;
Response:	**On the road to Bethlehem.**
Child Leader:	Be with us and hear us and lead us, O God;
Response:	**On the road to Bethlehem.**

Prayer

Child: Let us pray. As we make the journey to Bethlehem, we confess we have not always done our best. We have put rocks and bumps in the road with our selfishness. We have not listened to God's Word. We have not been as helpful to our parents and our teachers and our friends as we could be. We have not thought much about the sick and lonely people and tried to comfort them. We have wanted our own way a lot of the time. We are sorry for our selfishness and we want to do better.

Leader: Boys and girls, God has wrapped his arms around you with his forgiveness. To thank him for his goodness and his care for us, let us put our arms on each other's shoulders and pray the prayer he taught us to pray.

Response: Lord's Prayer *(unison)*

Scripture

Leader: Let us listen now to the story of the first journey to Bethlehem. Listen carefully to the story, because I will ask you a question when it is finished.

(Read Luke 2:1-20.)

Leader: Who remembers what the shepherds said to one another when the angel went away? *(let them answer)* "Let us go to Bethlehem and see this thing that has happened that the Lord has told us." Our children's choir will tell us more about this story.

Children's Choir Anthem

(Children's choir or church school class sings, "How Far Is It To Bethlehem?" or "How Many Miles To Bethlehem?" or "Shepherds, Shepherds, Where Are You Going?")

Action/Sermon

Leader: The road to Bethlehem is a long, long road. For many, many years, people had waited for a Savior to be born. We think of Christmas as the story of the birth of Jesus, and it is; but another way to think of Christmas is to remember some of the Old Testament stories and events leading up to the birth of Christ. Let's remember some of these people who traveled the long road to Bethlehem, waiting for a Savior.

(Congregation sings verse 1 of "Come, Thou Long-expected Jesus.")

Child 1: *(comes to the front carrying a figure and holds it up for the congregation to see)* Here is Abraham, the great forefather of the Hebrew people. He is thought to have lived about 2000 B.C. At the time of Abraham, most of the people of the world believed in many gods. Abraham came to believe that there was only one true God. One day, he heard the voice of God telling him to leave his home in the Arabian desert and travel westward to the land known as Canaan to make a new home there. He took all his family and possessions and made the long, hard journey. He walked to the promised land. He was waiting for a Savior. *(places figure on the table, then sits down)*

(Congregation sings verse 1 of "Come, Thou Long-expected Jesus.")

Child 2: *(comes to the front carrying a figure and holds it up for the congregation to see)* Here is Jacob, the grandson of Abraham. Once Jacob had a fight with his brother and ran away from home. Jacob traveled over valleys and mountains and through forests and fields. One night he was very weary and laid down to sleep under the open sky. He dreamed that a great ladder of light rose from the earth, its top reaching to heaven. On the highest rung stood God, who renewed to Jacob the promise he had made to Abraham that the land of Canaan should belong to their descendants. After many years, Jacob decided to return home. On the way home, God appeared to him and told him to change his name to Israel, and after that the Hebrews called themselves Israelites, or the children of Israel. Jacob was waiting for a Savior. *(places figure on the table, then sits down)*

(Congregation sings verse 1 of "Come, Thou Long-expected Jesus.")

Child 3: *(comes to the front carrying a figure and holds it up for the congregation to see)* Here is Joseph, Jacob's favorite son. Because of jealousy, his brothers sold him into slavery and he was carried off into the land of Egypt. After many hardships, he rose to a place of power in the Egyptian government. When a great famine hit the nation, Joseph forgave his brothers and brought them and his father and all of their families to live with him in Egypt. He spent his life trying to follow God, doing his best in a strange land, waiting for a Savior. *(places figure on the table, then sits down)*

(Congregation sings verse 1 of "Come, Thou Long-expected Jesus.")

Child 4: *(comes to the front carrying a figure and holds it up for the congregation to see)* Here is Moses. For 400 years, the children of Israel lived happily in Egypt. They prospered and increased, and then changes came about. A new pharaoh who hated the Hebrews and made them slaves, ruled over Egypt. The people suffered greatly. Moses led them out of Egypt into the wilderness. It was a hard life. They found no city to live in. They were hungry and thirsty and weary, but God was with them. In the desert, he gave Moses the

Ten Commandments and he always led them and fed them. For many years, they wandered about seeking the holy land that God had promised them. Moses died on a lonely mountain before the people entered the promised land. Moses had been given the Law, but he waited for truth and grace. He waited for a Savior. *(places figure on the table, then sits down)*

(Congregation sings verse 1 of "Come, Thou Long-expected Jesus.")

Child 5: *(comes to the front carrying a figure and holds it up for the congregation to see)* Here is David. After the Hebrews had settled in Canaan, he became their greatest king. He made Jerusalem the capital city. Here he brought the sacred chest containing the Ten Commandments. He built a tabernacle where it could be kept. David reigned for forty years, waiting for a Savior. *(places figure on the table, then sits down)*

(Congregation sings verse 1 of "Come, Thou Long-expected Jesus.")

Child 6: *(comes to the front carrying a figure and holds it up for the congregation to see)* Sad to say, the kingdom built up to such magnificence by David and his son, Solomon, was not to last. Enemies destroyed the cities and captured the people. During that time, men of godly spirit arose who believed that they were directed by God to lead their people back to the ways of righteousness. These great religious leaders were called prophets. The noblest of the prophets was Isaiah. He was filled with a sense of the greatness of God. He dreamed of a golden age when the ways of men would be the ways God had taught them, and all injustice and wrong would be swept away. He dreamed and taught and preached, waiting for a Savior. *(places figure on the table, then sits down)*

Leader: And the wonderful news we have to tell is that in the fullness of time, God *did* send a Savior; a child was born in Bethlehem who would show the world how to live. He would show them what God was really like. He would be like a light shining through the many years of dark waiting. It was as Isaiah had prophesied.

Child 6: "The people that walked in darkness have seen a great light. They that dwelt in the land of the shadow of death, upon them hath the light shined. For unto us a child is born, unto us a son is given and the government shall be upon his shoulders and his name shall be called Wonderful Counselor, the Mighty God, the Everlasting Father, the Prince of Peace" (Isaiah 9:2).

(Congregation sings verse 2 of "Come, Thou Long-expected Jesus.")

Presentation Of Gifts
Leader: The people who first came to the manger at Bethlehem brought gifts. The Wise Men brought gold and frankincense and myrrh. The shepherds brought lambs and piped a merry tune for the new baby. If we came to the manger, we might bring clothes to keep the baby warm. Since we can't go to Bethlehem, we can share those gifts with children here.

(Preschool children bring forward mittens to be given to a local day care center.)

Leader: If we came to the manger, we might bring toys. Since we can't go to Bethlehem, we can share those gifts with children here.

(Elementary children bring forward small toys.)

Leader: If we came to the manger, we might bring food. Since we can't go to Bethlehem, we can share those gifts with children here.

(Older elementary children bring forward canned goods.)

Leader: Accept these gifts, O Father. We bring them to Bethlehem remembering your words: "Inasmuch as you have done it unto one of the least of these, you have done it unto me."

Closing Hymn   "O Come, All Ye Faithful"

Producing Christmas

A Humorous
Children's Christmas Play

Jennifer Hockenbery Dragseth

Producing Christmas

Characters
Producer — three speaking
Mary — five speaking
Joseph — six speaking
Shepherd — five speaking
Angels — any number

There can be more of each of the characters with nonspeaking parts. The Producers should be sixth to eighth graders. The characters of Mary and Joseph should be third to fifth graders. The Shepherds should be kindergarteners through second graders. The part of the Angels should be three- to five-year-olds.

Props
Sunglasses
Megaphones
Producer's chair
Video camera

Processional Song   "O, Come Little Children"

Scene 1
(Producers dressed like Hollywood producers — sunglasses and the like)

Producer 1: I called you because the boss called and they want us to produce a holiday-season flick: "The Christmas Story."

Producer 2: "The Christmas Story" — that's been done already — about the kid who wants the gun but everyone's worried that he'll shoot his eye out?

Producer 1: No the actual Christmas story this time. The one in the Bible.

Producer 2: Oh yeah, the one with the Grinch and the Whos in Whosville — that's been done already, too.

Producer 3: Oh, that is a great story. I bet they made tons of money on it.

Producer 1: No, that's Dr. Seuss. Don't you know the difference between Dr. Seuss and Saint Luke? The Christmas story — it's about Jesus.

Producer 2: Oh, yes, now I remember — about Jesus hoarding all his money and then he's visited by the ghosts of Christmas past, present, and future.

Producer 3: And then he learns the true meaning of Christmas — having good friends and giving to charity.

Producer 1: That's not Jesus, that's Scrooge. Don't you know the Christmas story? The one about the birth of Jesus, the Son of God, born to a virgin, in a stable because there is no room in the inn? And wise people and shepherds come to worship him and the angels sing.

Producer 2: Oh, that Christmas story. Of course.

Song   "Joy To The World"

Scene 2
(Marys, Josephs, and Producers)

Mary 1: Is this where the tryouts are being held for the new movie? The one about Madonna?

Producer 1: Yes it is. It's going to be a real blockbuster.

Mary 2: Well, I should think so, with me as the lead.

Producer 3: Uh oh, I don't think you understand.

Producer 2: This is just the audition.

Mary 3: Oh, please. None of those other starlets have what it takes to be Madonna.

Producer 1: Um, do you know what this movie is about?

Mary 4: Sure! It's about making a lot of money and finally becoming a huge star! At last my big break!

Producer 3: I really don't think you understand.

Producer 2: No, it's about the birth of God as a human baby — a baby that is going to save the world.

Mary 5: Save the world? Oh, no, it's a guy movie — a Rambo thing? I won't be the main star, just an accessory? This stinks. I thought this was going to be my big break.

Joseph 1: Yes, I knew this was going to be a great movie.

Joseph 2: And with me as the lead actor.

Joseph 3: Not you, me. This is a role for a man with big muscles.

Producer 1: No, it's nothing like Rambo. It's about a baby, not a warrior. A tiny baby who is God.

Joseph 4: I'm not playing a baby.

Joseph 5: I think we are auditioning for the dad's part.

Joseph 6: Oh, I'm way too young to start playing a dad. I want to be the hero.

Producer 2: Didn't you read the script? It says right here in the lines of the angel: "Great joy to all people, for today in the city of David, a Savior is born to you. It is Christ the Lord, and this is a sign for you, you will find a baby wrapped in swaddling cloths and lying in a manger."

Mary 6: Wow, this is a wild script. No one will believe it.

Song   "The First Noel"

Scene 3

(Shepherds)

Shepherd 1: Wow, I can't believe I was picked to be in this new movie!

Shepherd 2: Me, either, I am so excited!

Shepherd 3: I have been practicing my karate moves all week — I can't wait to try them on the angels!

Shepherd 4: What are you talking about? We don't want to hurt the angels.

Shepherd 3: Sure we do, or else they will try to take over the world.

Shepherd 5: What are you talking about?

Shepherd 3: Right here, it says the angels make us tremble in terror.

Shepherd 1: But then the angels say, "Be not afraid, we have good news."

Shepherd 3: A trick to calm us before they try to grab us and take over the world.

Shepherd 2: Did you read the script?

Shepherd 4: I don't think you did. The angels sing beautiful songs and lead the shepherds to Jesus.

Shepherd 3: Well, that hardly sounds like a hit story line.

Shepherd 5: Ah, but it is! It's the best story line ever!

Shepherd 1: It's the story that God loves us so much that he comes to save them as a baby.

Song   "Go Tell It On The Mountain"

Scene 4

(Angels with Shepherds)

Shepherd 2: Here are the angels now. Shh. They are practicing their lines.

Angels:
Little Shepherd who watches sheep? *(put hand to forehead to watch)*
We, the angels, interrupt your sleep. *(point to self, then make sleepy hands on side of head)*
Wake up, we have good news to tell. *(put hands up, shake finger)*
God is born. All will be well. *(cradle pretend baby)*

Alleluia, Jesus is born. *(lift one finger)*
Blow your trumpet, blow your horn. *(put hands out like a horn)*
Alleluia, good news we bring. *(ring pretend bell)*
God comes to shepherds as well as kings. *(point to shepherds)*

Song   "Hark! The Herald Angels Sing"

91

Scene 5

(Producers and all)

Producer 1: All right. We are ready to start filming. Places everyone.

Producer 2: This is going to be a wonderful movie. We'll make millions!

Producer 3: I'm going to pick out my new Lexus tonight!

Mary 1: It will be wonderful, not because we make millions, but because it is a true story. A story beyond our wildest imaginations, but true nonetheless. A story about God coming to earth as a baby, who will grow up to teach us, lead us, die for us, and rise again promising us never-ending life.

Producer 2: All right, everybody. Let's start.

Producer 3: *(reads the Gospel of Luke)*

Song   "Away In The Manger"

A Christmas Journey

A Christmas Eve Service Of Candles And Carols

Rod Tkach

To Justin and Ben

*With fond memories of the boys you once were
and a father's pride in the men you've become.*

Introduction

"A Christmas Journey" engages the heart and imagination as we journey toward Christmas. The anticipation of "Are we there, yet?" is present in this candlelight service that features scripture readings, meditations, the lighting of the Advent candles, as well as congregational prayers and carols. If a congregation is blessed with musical talent, some of the carols may be featured as specials instead of being sung by the congregation. The number of people involved in the service is at your discretion. The anticipation gives way to the joy of arrival as the service climaxes with the singing of "Silent Night" by candlelight.

Order Of Service

Gathering Music

Welcome And Greeting
It is a joy to welcome you to our Christmas Eve service of candles and carols. May you sense the presence of God as we embark on a Christmas journey. Please stand as we turn to the call to worship printed in your bulletin.

Call To Worship
Leader: The road less traveled calls us.
People: If we are to journey to Christmas, this is the way.
Leader: Weeks of preparation gives way to the silence of the sanctuary.
People: The destination of the Christmas journey is here.
Leader: For the God who comes reveals Immanuel.
People: Come and worship Christ, the newborn king.

Christmas Carol   "Angels From The Realms Of Glory"

The First Step
Scripture Reading   Micah 5:2-5a

Meditation   "Home Alone For Christmas"

Lighting Of Advent Candle   Candle Of Presence
The evergreen of the Advent wreath symbolizes eternal life found in Christ. The candles signify God's Son as the light of the world. Advent is a time of prayerful preparation for the coming of Immanuel. This gift of "God with us" is symbolized in the first candle, the candle of God's *presence.*

Christmas Prayer

O God of Christmas, we get so caught up in our preparations for having family home for the holiday that we tune out those who are home alone. Forgive us, we pray. Give us the grace to share your love so that those who take the risk of entering here alone may receive the gift of fellowship; in Jesus' name. Amen.

Christmas Carol   "O Little Town Of Bethlehem"

The Second Step

Scripture Reading   Isaiah 9:2-7

Meditation   "The Rest Stop"

Lighting Of Advent Candle   Candle Of Hope
The second candle helps us to hear God's words: "Be still and know that I am God." In entering into the sanctuary of silence, we can also hear God say: "Taste and see that the Lord is good." It is when we pull off the interstate of our busyness to rest in his presence that our *hope* is renewed.

Christmas Prayer

Lord, how easy it is to rush past you as we hurry to get ready for Christmas. And then we encounter someone's act of kindness. Through it they show the courage to proclaim the good news to those who long to find their way home. By your lovingkindness enable us to practice your presence while sharing hope through acts of kindness. May we assist others as they travel the way to Immanuel, in whose name we pray. Amen.

Christmas Carol   "God Rest Ye Merry Gentlemen"

The Third Step

Scripture Reading   Isaiah 11:1-10

Meditation   "Trimming The Tree"

Lighting Of Advent Candle   Candle Of Love
The third candle shines upon the heart's quest to be right with God: "Will you pray for me?" Praying for another is an act of love. Continue praying, until they are ready to pray for themselves to receive the God who forgives and expresses the eternal realities of Christmas. *Love* is the light that prays.

Christmas Prayer
O God of love, how often we fail to see the sacred moments of life. But Christmas has a way of opening our hearts to new possibilities. You have love for the sinner gone wrong; for love came down at Christmas through your Son so we might become your adopted daughters and sons. Help us to move beyond the decorations to hear your invitation of love. Amen.

Christmas Carol   "Love Came Down At Christmas"

The Fourth Step

Scripture Reading   Matthew 2:1-2, 7-12

Meditation   "The Missing Jesus"

Lighting Of Advent Candle   Candle Of Faith
The fourth candle symbolizes the search for God. Many times we are told to seek God. The interesting thing is that through the search we discover that God has been seeking us! And that when we seek, he promises that we will find him. Such is the way of *faith.*

Christmas Prayer
The missing Jesus reminds us, Lord, of our need to seek you. This Christmas give us the childlike faith to embrace you. May you fill our heartfelt need to have Jesus with us. And then use us to help others find the Jesus missing from their lives, so they too may discover the Son of God, in whose name we pray. Amen.

Christmas Carol   "O Come, All Ye Faithful"

The Fifth Step
Receiving Of Christmas Offering
As the Magi journeyed to bring their gifts, so, too, we journey to bring our gifts. The monetary gifts are part of it, but so are our other gifts: the prayers of grateful hearts that rise like incense, the praise more precious than gold and myrrh or our pain turned to joy by the grace of Immanuel.
We call upon the ushers to receive the offering.

Offertory

The Sixth Step
Scripture Reading   Luke 2:1-14

Christmas Carol   "Hark! The Herald Angels Sing"

Meditation   "The Christmas Cross"

Christmas Prayer
The Christmas journey, O Lord, is one of you coming to us. But it is also one of us traveling to you. On this silent night, help us to see how you transform our darkness by the light of the cross; that as we sing of the cradle, we may experience the heart-changing miracle of God with us. Amen.

Lighting Of Advent Candle   Christ Candle

The center candle of the Advent wreath is the Christ candle. It reveals the heart of God as it is also the center candle of the cross. It is the holy light that overcomes the darkness as it reaches vertically to God and horizontally to others. We become light as the transforming light of Christ touches our hearts ... from the cradle to the cross, the story of God's love is told.

The Seventh Step
Lighting Of Individual Candles

Christmas Carol   "Silent Night"

Benediction

Our Christmas journey has brought us into the presence of the God who comes. In the silence of this holy night, go in the grace and peace of Immanuel. Amen.

Sending Music

Home Alone For Christmas

Those days in December had always been delightful. The expectation turning to anticipation as the children would migrate home for the holidays. First it was college that took them to distant destinations. That was bearable because breaks and summers guaranteed their frequent return. However, it didn't take a prophet to see that career and marriage would reduce those returns.

Then it happened: "I'll be home for Christmas" became "I wish I could, but...." After years of Christmases filled with children and presents, we were *home alone* for Christmas. At first, there wasn't any Christmas for the Grinch to steal, for it had all the makings of a blue Christmas. The well-wishers' "Merry Christmas" only intensified the feeling of loneliness. Maybe old Scrooge had it right after all!

There were no chestnuts on the open fire, but as the embers flickered their last, they sparked the thought, "untended fires soon die." Part of the pain of Christmas was not having family home, of being home alone. Would anyone venture into this world that was cold and gray instead of merry and bright? Would they see the tears or scurry away, embarrassed because of them? Would they see that there were only embers in the hearth of heart?

The cheer of *"I'll be home for Christmas"* came from unlikely sources. The teenager, with an infectious smile, bagging groceries. The store was a zoo, yet there was a serenity about him that touched my heart. The unexpected phone call from a friend from years gone by fanned the embers a little more. When asked what prompted the call, the reply came: "After all these years, the Lord brought you to mind. So I took a chance you might still be at this old number."

We went to the Christmas Eve service by ourselves, alone. At first it was tough to watch as families filled pews; a reminder of what was missing this Christmas. But that changed as we were swept up in the mystery and miracle of Christmas, the candles, and the carols working their magic. The memories of Christmas brought a smile. The last carol was sung by candlelight. And then we joined hands to pray. That's when we knew we were no longer home alone for Christmas!

The Rest Stop

The sun was peaking over the buttes as the mini-van was being loaded. The frigid winter air left little doubt that winter would once again cover the open prairies with a blanket of snow. Suitcases and presents were carefully stacked behind the backseat. The most precious cargo was still to come. Leaving the motor running gave the vehicle a chance to warm up as the children, bundled in blankets, were carried out and then buckled into place.

By mid-morning the backseat came to life. As noon drew closer the dreaded question grew louder: "Are we there yet?" Many more miles had to be conquered before the answer would be "Yes." About the time hunger set in, the arches appeared. While happy meals were being ordered, the play area absorbed excess energy. After burgers and fries, even the youngest fry was ready to be on the road again.

The sunlight began to disappear as we came upon a rest area out in the middle of nowhere. It was a welcome sight as the children were cranky. A mixture of aromas greeted us: the smell of coffee, hot apple cider, and fresh baked Christmas goodies. A hearty "Merry Christmas" came from a grandpa and grandma who served as hosts.

The children were elated, for this grandma's goodies were as good as their grandma's goodies! The visit lasted a few minutes, but it was long enough to learn their story. Since their grown children couldn't come home for Christmas, they decided to share a touch of Christmas with those who were traveling home. Yes, it took some doing to receive state permission, and it took a lot of work to do the baking. But the smiles and words of thanks they received from travelers were gifts they would take home. And what stories to tell when the phone calls were made to their children on Christmas Day!

Trimming The Tree

With each move, finding the perfect place for the Christmas tree was the post-Thanksgiving challenge. Sizes and styles of houses varied, but the size of the tree remained constant. Living far from family not only meant that the UPS man replaced Santa; it also meant that the arrival of presents was not limited to Christmas Eve. Indeed, the man in brown came early and there were hopes that he would also come often.

The only place to store gifts was under the tree. That meant that the tree had to be decked and trimmed for Christmas before that first visit from UPS. First one string of lights and then another were plugged in and carefully checked. The garland was carefully laid out across the back of the couch. Finally, the ornaments were gently removed from their boxes and arranged for all to see.

Before any lights were put on, before any ornaments were hung, or before any garland graced the tree, an old record was put on the stereo. It became a family tradition to listen before decorating. The song never ceased to work its magic. In it a little altar boy was asked to pray for a sinner gone wrong. It raises the question of what must one do to be holy?

The song put decorating in a different light. It made decorating a matter of the heart, an expression of love, something done as a gift to the Lord. It wasn't something to be conquered or to be crossed off the list. Rather, it became a way of embracing a sacred moment.

The Missing Jesus

Through a child's eyes, the weekend after Thanksgiving was magical. The house changed from a place where we lived to a Christmas wonderland. Outdoor decorations appeared as homes were trimmed in colorful lights. Inside, the Christmas tree was decorated while carols played on the stereo. Garland graced the banister while the stockings were hung over the fireplace. Christmas mugs replaced the coffee cups and the aromas of Christmas baking filled the house. There was just one thing left to do: the Nativity.

With great care, the pieces were unwrapped and set into place. The donkey and sheep would be rearranged countless times. The Magi were moved until their place was just right. Joseph and Mary were placed on either side of the manger. The final piece, the baby Jesus, was laid to rest in swaddling cloths. By evening, Jesus was missing!

An all-out search was launched. Every member of the family was assigned a specific area. There was a passionate determination to find the missing Jesus. After all, what good is a Nativity with no Jesus? What seemed like an eternity passed when an excited voice declared, *"I found him!"* Would you believe that Jesus was hiding in the plants?

This was the first of many searches for the missing Jesus. Sometimes we would find Jesus behind the recliners, other times under the pillow of our two-year-old, but mostly he had Jesus with him! That year a journey of spiritual significance was brought to life by a "missing Jesus." In the midst of all the preparations, we lost Jesus. But in seeking Jesus, we found the Son of God!

The Christmas Cross

Memories have a way of taking us back. Christmas memories have a way of taking us back to childhood. The Christmas Eve service was always special; especially since we boys were the only children involved. That's what happens when Dad's a pastor. It was tough to find an empty pew on Christmas Eve. The prelude gave way to the sound of silence as the altar candles were lit.

The service centered on a most unusual cross. The base of the white cross rested on the sanctuary floor and it had foldout legs that propped it up on the platform steps. The cross was ten feet long and six feet wide. It had funny little steps on it that were plant stands for Easter Lilies. All told, it held sixteen plants. It had never been done that way, but for Christmas that year the cross was trimmed in gold, the plant holders were draped in red felt, and were graced with white taper candles.

The service was one of candles and carols. At different points in the service, we would light a candle. The candlelighters were almost as tall as we were, so we used matches. There was always a nervousness with the worry about tripping or starting the cross on fire! The service's crescendo came as the center candle of the cross was lit. The verses of Immanuel's birth brought the cradle and the cross together. The holiness of Christmas became real at that moment.

From the Christ candle our candles were lit. We shared our light and soon candles throughout the congregation joined the chorus of light. "Silent Night" was prayerfully sung as the sanctuary lights were turned out. The Christmas story took on a deeper meaning as the light of the cross illuminated the heart of God in the midst of darkness. In those moments, time was touched by eternity and even as children we knew that something special happened: *God was with us!*

Christmas Letters

Christmas Eve Service Of Candles And Carols

Rod Tkach

To Dad

*As a Veteran's Service Officer, he exemplified the meaning
of honor expressed through compassion.*

*As a disciple of Jesus Christ, he lived out the meaning
of keeping the faith.*

*As a father, he demonstrated a love that
hoped, endured, and believed.*

Introduction

Christmas letters come in all shapes, sizes, and forms. The "Christmas Letters" candle light service combines carols, scripture, congregational prayers, meditations, and the lighting of the Advent candles as it brings Christmas letters to life. The service features a simple elegance as it delivers us into the presence of God.

The number of participants is flexible as two readers can alternate or a variety of people can be used to read the scripture, the meditation, and the Advent candle reading before the candle is lit. A song leader may be used but the Christmas carols are so well known that you may get by without one.

Ushers or other designated people will need to assist in the lighting of the individual candles. The more help in this area, the faster the lighting of the candles. Remind the congregation to hold their lighted candles upright and dip each unlighted candle into the flame of a lighted candle.

The Christmas carols featured in this service contribute to the flow of the service. If your congregation is blest with musical talent, then you have other options than congregational singing. Because the singing of the carols is so popular, we announce a couple of weeks in advance that the singing of carols will begin fifteen minutes before the service starts. The carols chosen are those that are not part of the service.

The service concludes with the singing of "Silent Night " in a candlelit sanctuary. Following the benediction, the lights are brought up and large baskets are placed by the exits for the collection of the individual candles.

Order Of Service

Gathering Music   Singing Of Christmas Carols

Welcome And Greetings

Call To Worship
Leader: What if God wrote a letter?
People: And Moses descended with two tablets written by God.
Leader: What if God wrote a letter?
People: And the Word of the Lord came to the prophets.
Leader: What if God wrote a letter to fulfill the law and the prophets?
People: Come to Bethlehem and see if such a letter comes special delivery.

Christmas Carol   "Angels From The Realms Of Glory"

Special Delivery
Scripture Reading   Isaiah 40:3-8

Meditation   "Christmas Letters"

Lighting Of Advent Candle   Candle Of Faith
     The Advent wreath reminds us that there is a time of *waiting* and *preparation* before we enter the land of Christmas. The candle of faith encourages us to look back and see how God has been faithful. It reminds us that the God who promises an advent is the one who comes. God shares his intention through the letter of his word. The first candle reminds us that God keeps his Word, thereby inspiring the light of faith.

Christmas Prayer

O Lord of Christmas, there is so much mail at Christmas as flyers, advertisements, and catalogues fill our mailboxes. The typical Christmas letter, sent or received, seldom helps us focus on faith. Faith may be there, but it's usually hidden between the lines. Forgive us for conveniently keeping our faith out of sight. Give us the grace to keep faith in the forefront this Christmas. In the name of the Christ. Amen.

Christmas Carol   "O Come, All Ye Faithful"

Delivered By UPS

Scripture Reading   Isaiah 35:1-6

Meditation   "Christmas Boxes"

Lighting Of Advent Candle   Candle Of Joy

Joy. It's uninhibited wonder. It's the awe inspired by a gift that makes the eyes dance. It's the exuberance and delight that makes the soul soar. In Bethlehem such a gift was delivered; a gift so precious that it was announced by angels. For through this gift, God provided the solution to humanity's sin problem. The second candle reminds us of the gift of God's presence in Christ.

Christmas Prayer

Most gracious God, we learn about giving from you. Help us to see the love behind each gift given this Christmas. Enable us to see beyond the gift to the joy of the one who gives. May that thoughtfulness and joy warm our hearts. Help us, O Lord, with all the giving and gifts to have hearts filled with childlike wonder at the gift you have given in Christ. Amen.

Christmas Carol   "Hark! The Herald Angels Sing"

The Christmas Wait

Scripture Reading   Luke 1:26-35, 38

Meditation   "Waiting For Christmas"

Lighting Of Advent Candle   Candle Of Love
Waiting. That's what the love of God does. He has been waiting for us to come to him. The third candle is the candle of love. We might get impatient for Christmas to come or be tempted to rush right through it. But this candle reminds us to wait, to be still in God's presence; for it is then that we experience the God who comes, the very God who has been waiting for us to receive his gift of love in Immanuel.

Christmas Prayer
O Lord, we anxiously wait for Christmas to come. While it seemingly takes forever, time quickly slips by. In the hustle and bustle of preparations, it is easy not to take the time to be in your presence, to ponder the mystery and miracle of your coming, or to be wrapped in the wonder of your love.
Forgive us, we ask. And give us the grace to first experience and then share your love in the fullness of this time of Christmas. Amen.

Christmas Carol   "Love Came Down At Christmas"

Their Arrival Said It All

Scripture Reading   Matthew 1:18-25

Meditation   "Letters From Home"

Lighting Of Advent Candle   Candle Of Hope
It is one of the principles of life that spurs us to action and guides us through life's journey. It is represented in the fourth candle, the candle of hope. *Hope* expresses the deepest of the desires of the heart and the longings of the soul. It goes to the core of life's

meaning. Without hope we are prone to question whether life is worth living. This candle reminds us that our hope rests in the one born in Bethlehem.

Christmas Prayer
When we are far from home, O Lord, hope can seem so distant. But being far from home can be more than a matter of geography. It can be a matter of the heart. We need to find our way home, not only in terms of family but also in our relationship with you.

Help us to hear your word; that through the gift of Jesus there is hope for us. May the hopes and fears of all the years be met in you this night. Amen.

Christmas Carol   "O Little Town Of Bethlehem"

Letters That Give
Receiving Of Christmas Offering
How often as children do we open the mail and shake the card to see if there is any money? You, O Lord, spared no expense in sending your Son. Bless these gifts, we pray, that others may come to know the richness of life in Christ. Amen.

Offertory

The Ultimate Letter
Scripture Reading   John 1:1-5, 14

Meditation   "The Letter Is Sent"

Lighting Of Advent Candle   Christ Candle
"The letter is in the mail," was just not good enough for God. This letter was special delivery, taken care of personally. The Christ candle reminds us that God was in Christ *reconciling* the world to himself. The joy of Christmas with its faith, joy, love, and hope is fulfilled in the Christ who comes to hearts who receive him still.

Christmas Prayer

We give you thanks, O God, for the special delivery on a Christmas so long ago. It is humbling to think that you could love us that much. A letter written on stone would not do, nor would a letter spoken through the prophets. Instead, you sent the most unusual letter: your Son. May he light up our lives, we pray. Amen.

Christmas Carol   "What Child Is This?"

The Letter Is Being Sent

Scripture Reading   2 Corinthians 3:2-3

Meditation   "A Christmas Letter Revealed"

Lighting Of Candles   Congregational Candles

The Christmas story begins with God sending his Son, but the story does not end there as we, too, are God's letters. Let the love of God's letter shine through you as your light comes from the Christ candle to the ushers to you. After all the candles are lit, we will sing the first verse of "Silent Night" and then listen in silence as the organ and piano play the last verse.

Christmas Carol   "Silent Night"

Benediction

O God, it was through the letters of the lives of others that we first came to learn of your personal letter to us in Christ Jesus. Their lives opened your letter of salvation to us. As we celebrate the birth of Immanuel, may your Spirit use our lives to be letters that invite others to experience new life in Christ. We ask it in the name of the Living Letter, Jesus our Lord. Amen.

Sending Music

Christmas Letters

Neither snow nor rain nor gloom of night stays these couriers from the swift completion of their appointed rounds. Most of the year the children are oblivious to the mail. But, as Christmas approaches, the mail takes on great significance. With the arrival of the catalogues, the dreaming begins.

Not everything in the mail generates such joy. The envelopes graced with Christmas décor meet the same fate as the plain white ones: a carol of sighs complete with a refrain of moans. The children dismiss them with a frosty dismay: "We don't even *know* these people. Do we have to read the letters as a family?"

It takes time to appreciate the Christmas letter ritual. As the years pass, the children begin to identify certain styles with certain names. There's "so and so" whose family letter is like Lake Wobegone fiction. Then there's the travelogue letter with its extensive itinerary with places we recognize and lists of people that leave us asking, "Who are they?" Then there's one that the others can't hold a candle to. Unlike form letters, this one is concise and it's verse is poetic. It's entertaining and fun to read.

So what makes a Christmas letter "special"? It's the one time of the year that we make the effort to contact people who are dear to our hearts. It is an investment of ourselves in the lives of others. That handwritten note on the bottom or the back of the form letter makes it personal. The Christmas letter helps hold us together. Without it, some would just drift apart.

But the Christmas letter can be so much more than a recital of the year's highlights. The best Christmas letters affirm a love that tells faith's story. They own up to life's disappointments, shattered dreams, and the seemingly unanswered prayers, but they do it in a way that, in spite of it all, shows how God has been faithful. They do it in a way that hangs on to God's promises. After all, there were years of waiting before the promise of Christ's coming was fulfilled. That's the faith conveyed by the best Christmas letters.

Christmas Boxes

The voice on the television commercial asks, "What can Brown do for you?" There is no hesitation as the children reply, "Come to our house!" When the UPS truck shows up in December, it means one thing and one thing only: presents!

One never knows what size the box will be or from what part of country it comes. It might be a cereal box from the prairies, a paper products box from the great northwest, or a singer's sausage box from the south. It's all a mystery until it's brought to the door. A quick check of the label identifies the sender. But, wait, he's bringing another box!

The excitement is not dimmed by the task at hand; that is, cutting through the tape. For it seems that some in the family take great delight in making sure that the package, would not and could not, accidentally open. How many roles of duct tape, strapping tape, and packing tape were used remains a mystery. Regardless of the size of the box or the amount of tape used, one thing remained certain. Hidden inside were individually wrapped presents, each with a nametag.

The children's eyes would light up as the pocketknife sliced through the tape revealing the treasures within. Even though the individual gifts could not be opened until Christmas, it was a joy to place them under the tree. With each stop of the UPS truck, the open space under the tree became smaller.

Some might say that this is what is wrong with Christmas; that it's a spending spree spurred by greed and financed by plastic. It can be that if we let it. But inside those boxes were gifts of joy as the miles that separated family melted away. Those giving the gifts participated in the joy as phone calls expressed the excitement and appreciation.

The joy of the gifts came out of hearts filled with love. One can't help but wonder if we can't catch a glimpse of God's joy as he gave his most precious gift, his Son, to the world.

Waiting For Christmas

Christmas was a little more than a month away the day it came priority mail. Because it was so light, the children were convinced that it was nothing more than an empty envelope. As they opened it, a note fell to the floor. It read, "To help you *wait* for Christmas. Love, Grandma."

The Advent calendar helped the children wait as each day a door on the calendar was opened revealing another verse of the Christmas story. It kept the children focused on the scriptures as the countdown continued to build up to that much-anticipated day.

Waiting — it can be unbearable, especially when it's something the heart longs for. A grown-up's anxious pacing or mindless paging through a magazine to a child's inability to sit still or constantly asking, "Is it time?" are signs that the waiting is getting the best of us. The Advent calendar is a reminder that God waited until just the right time. Then the Angel Gabriel stepped into our time with a word: one for Mary and another for Joseph.

That word resulted in more waiting — nine months to be exact. Then in the fullness of time, the mystery and miracle happened. God didn't send a memo filled with theological jargon that wouldn't make sense to ordinary folk. God didn't send a note filled with insider phrases. He didn't send a dossier filled with fancy formulas.

Why wait till the fullness of time? From our point of view, waiting can be anxiety driven or it can be an opportunity to quiet our hearts before God. The latter combines a deep sense of helplessness with a complete confidence that God will work through his divine power. It is through this kind of waiting that we discover the mystery of the miracle that defies our imagination and yet entices it, that puzzles the mind, and yet allures it to explore.

This kind of waiting opens the door for God to come in the fullness of our time. It allows for his advent as the love of God could conceive of no greater way to express his redeeming love than to become one of us. The waiting of the Advent season prepares us for the God who comes.

Christmas Letters From Home

A soldier serving in Iraq noted that "Mail has secret powers that are felt most by those farthest removed. I would like to let you know how much your letter means to me." That is especially true at Christmas even if it was another place and another time. This is Ted Gibson's story.

Ted was in the Repair Squadron of the Fifth Air Force Group. They were on their way to Ohio's Wright Field when Japan attacked Pearl Harbor. Ten days, that's what they had to settle their personal affairs before shipping out. Their point of destination changed to Australia when the Philippines fell to the Japanese.

An International Harvest plant was transformed to assemble fighter planes. A foundry enabled them to make necessary parts using broken and bent propellers for raw materials. The group was transferred north of Melbourne where they waited for several months. Once things caught up with them, they were on the move once more. After the Battle of Coral Sea, the Philippines became their destination once again.

Typically, mail was sixty to ninety days late, but the months turned into a year with no word from home. Ted was feeling desperate. Why haven't they written? Have they forgotten me? If so, is life really worth living? Pondering these questions only deepened the despair.

Was there any reason to hope? At the deepest moment of despair, three words brought hope: You've got mail! Oh, it was not just one letter from home. It wasn't even double digit letters. Would you believe that it was 200? Oh, the secret powers of the mail worked a miracle.

Hope reached across the miles and gave a reason for living. Hope pointed beyond the immediate circumstances to something greater: a love that transcended the miles of separation. Hope had compelled Ted to hang on, to seek meaning in life when none was apparent. And when it seemed most hopeless, letters from home came *on Christmas Eve!*

The arrival of the letters pointed to something beyond the letters themselves. Faith is the *assurance of things hoped for* and the *conviction of things not seen.* Biblical hope is directed to God, trusting in his nature and his promises.

The long-awaited coming of the Messiah is our letter from home. Only hope gained from the Eternal is eternal. Through the birth, death, and resurrection of Christ, God offers us a hope that reaches through our despair while making the distance that separates us from him disappear.

The soldier's Christmas letters from home renewed hope; there was someone waiting for him at home. That first Christmas letter, of the Word made flesh, not only tells us that someone is waiting, but it shows us the way home.

The Letter Is Sent

How many times have you heard, "The letter is in the mail"? If it's in the mail, why does it take so long to show up? That is, if it shows up at all. The chances for mishap are many; from insufficient postage, to an incorrect address or the recipient having moved with no forwarding address being left, to the letter simply getting lost in the system.

How many times do we say, "The letter is in the mail"? We wait until the last possible moment to get it in the mail. Why? So there's enough in the account to make sure that the check is covered. Sometimes there is just too much month at the end of the money. The postmark becomes a matter of strategy. Get it there in time to avoid late fees but late enough that funds are sufficient.

Then the mail comes and along with it a moment of frustration. The one letter we hoped to avoid is right there on top. Its clear cellophane window tells us more than we want to know. Opening it, we are greeted with a reminder that our account is past due. So as not to be offensive there is a disclaimer: *If your payment and our letter crossed in the mail, please disregard this reminder.* Of course they crossed in the mail. It was mailed just before the mail arrived!

The Almighty didn't take any chances with his letter: for the Word became flesh and dwelt among us! His is a personal letter who comes to seek and to save that which is lost. His letter seeks us! Regardless of how many times we move, his letter keeps coming!

God's letter is the most unique in all the world. It informs us of our insufficient funds when trying to pay for our sins. It is impossible to buy our salvation. In the darkness of this despair, God intervenes. In the fullness of time, Jesus was born. His grace is more than sufficient as he provides the way to God the Father.

The lighting of the Christ candle reminds us that God delivered as promised: for today in the city of David there has been born for you a Savior, who is Christ the Lord. Not only that, God continues to deliver through the Christ who comes even now.

A Christmas Letter Revealed

The story of Christmas is incomplete; that is, the Christmas letter is not finished. But, you say, we've read God's letter. Jesus was born in Bethlehem, just as God said. So, in what possible sense could the Christmas letter be unfinished?

Glad you asked. It's unfinished in this way. The Apostle Paul tells the believers in Corinth, "You are our letter, written in our hearts, known and read by all men. [It is revealed] that you are a letter of Christ, cared for by us, written not with ink, but with the Spirit of God, not on tablets of stone, but on tablets of human hearts."

You, who believe that Jesus is the Christ and have gathered to worship, are God's letter. You may be a letter of faith that can inspire or a letter of joy that empowers someone to embrace life once again. You may be a letter of love that is unwrapped as you share your heart or a letter of hope whose power of presence comforts as it points to the promise of eternal life in Christ.

You are God's Christmas letter. The Christmas adventure continues as you let the light of Christ shine on this silent night, on this holy night.

About The Authors

Alan E. Siewert is a former Lutheran pastor and microbiologist who is the author of six children's books. A graduate of Capital University and Trinity Lutheran Seminary in Columbus, Ohio, he now enjoys working in many capacities as a lay minister and doing research in various fields.

H. Michael Nehls is the former pastor of St. Martin's Lutheran Church in Archbold, Ohio, and First Lutheran Church in Findlay, Ohio. He currently serves as the director of gift and estate planning for Grand View College in Des Moines, Iowa. Nehls is a graduate of Capital University and Trinity Lutheran Seminary.

Judy Gattis Smith is the author of more than a dozen books, including *Teaching the Mystery of God to Children* (CSS), *Teaching to Wonder*, *Planting Spiritual Seeds*, and *Developing a Child's Spiritual Growth through the Senses* (Abingdon). She has also written three books for grandmothers, and she is a regular contributor to *Episcopal Teacher* magazine. Smith has led more than 200 workshops and seminars, and has been a keynote speaker at conferences throughout the United States.

Jennifer Hockenbery Dragseth is an assistant professor of philosophy at Mount Mary College. She is a graduate of Bowdoin College and Boston University, where she wrote her Ph.D. dissertation on Saint Augustine's doctrine of grace. She is married to David Dragseth, who currently pastors Lake Park Lutheran Church in Milwaukee, Wisconsin.

Rod Tkach is a "prairie wordsmith" and the pastor of Faith United Methodist Church in Williston, North Dakota. He is a graduate of Jamestown College, Asbury Theological Seminary, and Southern Baptist Theological Seminary.

www.ingramcontent.com/pod-product-compliance
Lightning Source LLC
LaVergne TN
LVHW021520080426
835509LV00018B/2568